GW00993197

Puppy Training

How to Train Your puppy:
The ultimate guide for beginners on
raising your a puppy with positive
dog training basics. (Includes potty
& leash training).

Danny Wager

Table of Contents

INTRODUCTION..1

Chapter 1: Learning about Dog Breeds 11

Chapter 2: Choosing a Dog...17

Chapter 3: Bringing Your Puppy Home................................40

Chapter 4: Conditioning Your Puppy 52

Chapter 5: A Dog's Temperament..60

Chapter 6: Prepare For Training 67

Chapter 7: Basic Obedience Training...................................79

Chapter 8: Advanced Obedience Training 89

Chapter 9: Crate Training 95

Chapter 10: Housetraining..100

Chapter 11: Common Behavioral Problems.......................112

CONCLUSION..131

INTRODUCTION

The joy of bringing a new puppy or dog into your household can be insurmountable. After all, there is no relationship quite like the one that is developed between you and your dog.

A dog can provide unconditional love, hours of entertainment, and genuine friendship. Or, a dog can provide unconditional messes, hours of destruction, and a genuine nuisance!

How do you ensure that your dog behaves in the manner of the first scenario described above? If you are thinking that the answer is "breed" you are partially correct. Indeed, breed does play a role in a dog's behavior. But an even greater factor in the dog's behavior is based on the training he receives.

A dog's personality is largely contributed to what he experienced in his early puppy days. If he was mistreated by his owner, he will probably grow up to be shy, fearful, or aggressive towards people. If he is happy, energetic, and curious, he was probably handled with care during his early life.

The level of training that your dog has received will be partly determined by his age. Maybe you are receiving a brand new puppy that is under two months old. Maybe you are adopting a dog from an animal shelter and you are not exactly sure how old he is. Or, perhaps your dog is a couple of years old and he has already had basic training, and now you want to teach him some advanced training techniques.

No matter what level of training your dog needs—from the brand new puppy to the wise old dog—you need to consider some basic training techniques. This is the best way to ensure that you will have a healthy, happy, trusting relationship. This relationship could last well over a decade, so the better prepared you are with training, the better your relationship will be.

This E-book will provide you with many of these essential training techniques. Most will apply to your specific situation with your dog, others you may find that your dog is already a pro at, and others you may find that your dog isn't quite ready for yet.

The Benefits of Training

If you are like most people, you are extremely busy. Some days, there just doesn't seem like enough hours to take care of yourself, let alone a dog! But, the time that you spend training your dog will reward you and your relationship for many, many years to come.

There are five main benefits of training:

- It builds a relationship.
- It corrects behavioral problems.
- It stimulates intellect.
- It encourages inclusion.
- It saves time.

Let's explore each benefit in further detail.

1. Training Builds a Relationship.

There is no better way to create a bond with your dog than through the process of training. You may think that training begins at the time you decide to try new tricks, but it actually begins at the very moment you acquire your dog.

Your dog is constantly watching you and learning from your actions. He learns from the way you react to his actions. He looks to you for guidance, for food, for warmth, for comfort, and for playtime. So how do you build a healthy relationship with your dog? It depends on one essential element: mutual trust.

In order for training to be effective, your dog must trust you and you must trust your dog. Without trust, neither one of you can truly depend on the other. Without trust, there will always be a twinge of fear. Without trust, there will always be an element of uncertainty.

On the other hand, a relationship built on trust will instill confidence in each other. This confidence means that you trust your dog will come to you when you say "come." Your dog will be confident that when he comes to you, he will be rewarded.

When you and your dog are confident in each other, you allow each other to grow. For instance, the more that you can trust your dog to follow your commands, the more likely you are to teach him more and more commands.

When you establish a bond built on trust and confidence, you will need to nourish and strengthen that bond every day. This can be achieved by constantly reinforcing the training lessons. Don't just train a new command for a single week and then suddenly stop. Make it a habit to continually reinforce the training as often as you can.

The training exercises with your dog should not only be performed often, but they should also be consistent. That means if you teach the "stay" command one particular way, you should always practice it the same way. Using different "stay" commands will only confuse your dog and could even encourage distrust in your relationship. An interesting thing to point about training is, is that you are not only training your dog, but your dog is training you too! This is important to remember. He is training you how to react to his behaviors. And, he is training you how to be patient!

Without a doubt, the relationship you have with your dog must be based on trust. It may take awhile to build this trust, but once you do, you will see the rewards. Your dog will want to please you with good behavior, as will you want to please your dog with love, attention, treats, and playtime!

2. Training Corrects Behavioral Problems.

Barking at anyone who passes by the front window, chewing up your favorite pillows, digging through your freshly planted garden, bolting out of an open door...do any of these actions look familiar to you?

The second main benefit to training is that it can correct those pesky behavioral problems that your dog can't seem to give up. For him, these behaviors are ways to release frustration, break boredom, or even provide entertainment!

When you have developed a trusting bond with your dog, you can teach him how to correct these behavioral problems. He will learn by your reactions whether or not his actions are acceptable to you. No doubt, he will test his limits!

The process of training gives you the appropriate platform to correct his annoying and even destructive behavior. If training is not a part of your dog's life, you can expect the behavioral problems to continue. If training is a part of your dog's life, you can expect behavioral problems to be replaced with desirable behavior—as well as pillows in one piece and well-manicured gardens!

Chapter 11 will go into further detail about common behavioral problems and how to correct them.

3. Training Stimulates Intellect.

Yes, it is true that dogs are very curious creatures. With exposure to so many unusual smells, sights, and sounds, dogs can't help but want to explore. It's in their nature!

Most dogs have the capacity to be very intelligent. But, they need to be stimulated first, and then they will be motivated to learn. Training is a huge benefit for stimulating your dog's intellect. Just think about it from your dog's perspective. The opportunity to spend time with his owner, learn new tricks, and receive treats! Who wouldn't want to learn with such yummy rewards at stake?

When you take the time to train your dog, you are giving him a wonderful opportunity to not only pique his curiosity, but to expand his capacity to learn, and to increase his knowledge about his livelihood.

The more you train your dog, the more you will be surprised by his amazing intellect. Just see for yourself!

4. Training Encourages Inclusion.

The sense of "inclusion" is very important to a dog's security. From the earliest days of being a part of a litter, your dog feels comfortable being a part of the pack. That includes the pack of your household.

You may be the primary dog trainer, but everyone in your family or household should take the time to train your dog. When he receives this undivided attention from everyone, he feels like part of the pack. It was earlier mentioned that consistent training is required to ensure the trust of your dog. This not only means consistent training from you, but from everyone in your household. If everyone is going to take part in training, everyone should use the same methods.

For starters, as you read this E-book, highlight the sections that are relevant to you and the training methods that you want to implement with your dog. Then, have each member of your household read this E-book. When everyone devotes training time with the dog, the dog will be happy and more eager to learn and please his family!

5. Training Saves Time.

Another huge benefit of training your dog is that it saves you time. Taking the time to train your dog now, will actually save you time in the long run. For example, if you take the time to train your dog to behave properly inside the house, you will actually be saving time cleaning up mischievous messes that he could create in the future—if he didn't have the training.

You do not need to spend several hours a day training your dog. In fact, if you spend too much time training without a break, your dog could get easily distracted or bored, making it less effective.

Training for 30-60 minutes a day is adequate. You can break up this time throughout the day. Shorter sessions are actually better for optimum attention span. Plus, it is better to end the training session while your dog is still having fun. This way, he will anxiously await his next session. So, by simply scheduling time into your day, you will find that training your dog will be time well spent. These will be times that you and your dog will look forward to everyday!

Your Dog's Name

This may or may not be a surprise to you, but your dog's name is a very valuable training tool. Your dog needs to understand that when he hears his name, he needs to pay attention to what you are about to say or do.

If you are acquiring a puppy, he may not have a name yet. Or, maybe you are adopting a dog from a dog shelter and his name is unknown. In these cases, you will want to give your dog a name right away—as soon as the perfect name comes to mind.

Your dog will not realize what his name is, until you teach him. At first, he will only recognize his name as just a sound. So to teach your dog his name, repeat this exercise several times throughout the day:

- Say his name.
- When he looks at you, say "yes!" and
- Praise him or reward him immediately. After some practice, he will soon make the association that his name means something to be excited about!

For this reason, be careful to never say your dog's name when he does something wrong. This is difficult, because your natural reaction when catching your dog in the act of making an accident inside the house is "Rover, no! Bad dog!" *(Throughout this E-book, you will see the name "Rover" used for the commands. Obviously, you will replace "Rover" with your own dog's name.)*

When you use your dog's name to reprimand him, he will associate his name with "bad" or "punishment." These thoughts put fear in hearing his name, which is extremely counterproductive for the training process.

So, only use your dog's name when he can expect good things to happen. You want your dog to love the sound of his name!

Preparing Yourself for Training

It is no secret that training your dog is a lot of work—a lot of hard work. But that shouldn't discourage you. Actually, it should encourage you! Because by training your dog, you will be setting the stage for a mutually beneficial relationship.

There are five traits that you as a trainer can exhibit to ensure smooth training. It's not always easy to demonstrate these traits, but the more you do the more enjoyable and productive your training will be.

Five Traits for Training:

1. Confidence.

Indeed, training your dog can be intimidating, especially if you have never trained a dog before. But by using this E-book as a reference to help you learn how to train, you can gain the knowledge and the confidence you need for successful training.

If you are not confident when you are training your dog, he will be able to pick up on that sense of uncertainty. And if you don't have confidence in yourself, why should your dog have confidence in you?

When you are confident with your training, your dog will respect you as a leader and will learn his lessons faster.

2. Attitude.

The success of your training will also be determined by your attitude. You may be frustrated with your dog because of his destructive or disobedient behavior, but if you taint the training with your negative attitude, the training will be unsuccessful.

If you go into the training with a positive and energetic attitude, your dog will pick up on this and reciprocate back to you! Just remember, attitude is the one thing you can control in an uncontrollable situation. So if you had a bad day at work and came home to a mess, don't release your anger during your dog's training. Instead, adopt a positive attitude and you and your dog will enjoy the training experience.

3. Commitment.

Training your dog is a big time commitment and an emotional commitment. If you are really busy at work and putting in extended hours, you may be too tired at the end of the day to commit to training right now. It is better to wait until you have the time and energy to devote to training.

Once you decide you are ready to start training your dog, make a firm commitment with yourself that you will stick to it. Your training will only be effective if you set aside the time to do it.

4. Effort.

Once you have made the time commitment to train your dog, you need to give it your best effort. Training is not something that you can do half-heartedly; it needs to be done whole-heartedly.

Basically, remember this rule of thumb: The less effort you put into training your dog, the less progress you will see. The more effort you put into training your dog, the more responsive he will be to it and the more progress you will see.

5. Patience.

Patience. Patience. Patience. You will need a lot of it as you train your dog! There will be times when your dog would rather play than train. Or, he may be distracted by other activities going on inside the house. But, practice patience and you can actually find a sense of humor in his charming little idiosyncrasies!

It is worth noting that these five traits are not only important for you to exhibit, but they are also important for anyone in your household who is contributing to the training of your dog. Essentially, your family has welcomed your dog into the home, so it is up to everyone to be in agreement about the training goals, the training practices, and the training outcomes. When you do this, your family will be uniting with each other and increasing the quality of life for everyone—including your dog!

Chapter 1:
Learning about Dog Breeds

You may or may not know this, but there are literally hundreds of different types of dog breeds! A breed is a group of similar types of dogs with comparable psychological and physical characteristics.

Breeds are generally grouped together based on their uses for which they were originally developed. Most dog breeds are the result of artificial selection by human breeders.

Below is an extensive list of breeds, divided into six main groups: Working Dogs, Terriers, Hunting Dogs, Companion Dogs, Toys, and Greyhounds.

Some dog associations such as the American Kennel Club, the Australian National Kennel Council, and the United Kennel Club may have slight variations of the groupings, and may even include more groups. For example, the American Kennel Club includes the groups Sporting, Hound, Non-sporting, and Herding.

With so many breeds to choose from, it can be intimidating for someone searching for a dog breed that would be suitable for their family. There are several options available to help you learn about the specific dog breeds. Resources in the library and on the World Wide Web offer thousands of books and articles on the different breeds.

For more "hands on" learning, you could attend a dog show to see a wide variety of breeds. Of course, owners of these dogs typically take training much more seriously than the average dog owner; however, they tend to have extensive knowledge about their breed.

Once you have a few different breeds in mind, you could call or visit breeders with the possibility of seeing the dogs used for breeding. Other ideas are to visit veterinary offices, dog training schools, your local humane society, and even pet stores! Talking with people in parks or pet stores that allow dogs is interesting and fun because dog owners almost always love to talk about their precious dogs—to anyone!

Working Dogs

Dogs in the Working Group traditionally serve many purposes such as herding, guarding, pulling sleds, and aiding in water rescues. These dogs are usually larger in size and their intelligence enables them to learn quickly.

Working dogs are protective companions, but because of their strength, they may not all be appropriate for all families.

Breeds in the Working Group include:

Aidi	Akita Inu
Alaskan Malamute	Anatolian Shepherd Dog
Appenzell Mountain Dog	Australian Cattle Dog
Australian Kelpie	Australian Shepherd
Austrian Short-haired Pinscher	Bearded Collie
Beauceron	Belgian Malinois
Belgian Sheepdog	Belgian Tervuren
Bergamasco	Bernese Mountain Dog
Border Collie	Bourvier Des Ardennes
Bouvier Des Flandres	Boxer
Briard	Brindle Boxer
Brindle Great Dane	Bullmastiff
Canaan Dog	Cao Da Serra Da Estrela
Cao Da Serra De Aires	Cao De Castro Laboreiro
Catahoula Leopard Dog	Catalan Sheepdog
Collie	Croatian Sheepdog
Doberman Pinscher	Dutch Sheepdog
Entlebucher Sennenhund	Eskimo Dog
Fila Brasileiro	French Mastiff
German Shepherd	Giant Schnauzer
Great Dane	Great Pyrenees

Great Swiss Mountain Dog	Greenland
Harlequin Great Dane	Hokkaidoken
Hovawart	Iceland Dog
Illyrian Sheepdog	Karst Sheepdog
Keeshond	Komondor
Kuvasz	Kyushu
Landseer	Lapphund
Lapponian Herder	Leonberger
Long-haired St. Bernard	Maremma Sheepdog
Mastiff	Mudi
Neopolitan Mastiff	Newfoundland
Norrbottenspets	Norsk Buhund
Old English Sheepdog	Picardy Sheepdog

Terriers

Dogs in the Terrier Group vary in size from small to big, yet they are all boast a lot of bravery, determination, and energy. The earliest terriers were originally bred to hunt and kill vermin.

Most terriers can be identified with their wiry coats and big personalities! Because they have so much energy, it is important for their owners to be able to keep up with them.

Breeds in the Terrier Group include:

Airedale Terrier	American Staffordshire Terrier
Bedlington Terrier	Bohemian Terrier
Border Terrier	Boston Terrier
Bull Terrier	Cairn Terrier
Dandie Dinmont Terrier	German Hunting Terrier
Glen of Imaal Terrier	Irish Terrier
Jack Russell Terrier	Kerry Blue Terrier
Lakeland Terrier	Manchester Terrier
Norfolk Terrier	Norwich Terrier
Scottish Terrier	Sealyham Terrier
Skye Terrier	Smooth Fox Terrier

Soft-Coated Wheaten Terrier	Staffordshire Bull Terrier
Tibetan Terrier	Welsh Terrier
West Highland White Terrier	Wirehaired Fox Terrier

Hunting Dogs

Many of the breeds listed below were originally used for hunting, but as our society has become more urban, needs have changed. People tend to use many of these breeds as companions, including:

American Foxhound	Field Spaniel
Anglo-Francais Tricolor	Finnish Spitz
Austrian Hound	French Pointer
Barbet	Gammel Dansk Honsehund
Basset Artesian Normand	German Short-haired Pointer
Basset Fauve De Bretagne	German Wiredhaired Pointer
Basset Hound	Gordon Setter
Beagle	Grand Bleu De Gascogne
Bernese Hound	Grand Griffon Vendeen
Black and Tan Coonhound	Griffon Fauve De Bretagne
Bloodhound	Grosser Munsterlander
Bosnian Hound	Hamilton Hound
Braque d'Auvergne	Harrier
Braque Du Bourbonnais	Irish Setter
Braque Saint-German	Italian Hound
Briquet Griffon Vendeen	Jura Hound
Chesapeake Bay Retriever	Kleiner Munsterlander
Cirneco Dell'etna	Levesque
Clumber Spaniel	Long-haired Dachshund
Dachsbracke	Norwegian Elkhound
Drever	Perdiguero De Burgos
English Cocker Spaniel	Petit Anglo-Francais
English Setter	Petit Griffon Bleu De Gascogne

Companion Dogs

A companion dog is one that is not bred to work, but instead provides companionship as a pet. Really, any dog in any group can be a companion dog, including:

Belgian Griffon	Bichon Avanese
Bolognese	Cavalier King Charles Spaniel
Chow Chow	Dalmatian
English Bulldog	French Bulldog
Great Spitz	Griffon Brabancon
Hairless Dog	Harlekinpinscher
Japanese Spitz	Kromfohrlander
Miniature Schnauzer	Pinscher
Poodle	Pug
Schipperkee	Shar-pei
Shiba Inu	Small Spitz
Telomian	Tibetan Spaniel
Volpino Italiano	

Toys

The Toy Group consists of dogs smaller in size and they are sometimes considered an "accessory." **The Toy Group includes:**

Affenpinscher	Australian Silky Terrier
Australian Terrier	Bichon Frise
Black and Tan Toy Terrier	Brussles Griffon
Chihuahua	Chinese Crested Dog
Chinese Impreian Ch'in	Chinese Temple Dog
Coton De Tulear	English Toy Spaniels
Japanese Spaniel	Lhasa Apso
Little Lion Dog	Maltese
Mexican Hairless Dog	Papillon
Pekingese	Pomeranian
Shih-tzu	Silky Terrier

Small Continental Spaniel	Toy Fox Terrier
Toy Terrier	Yorkshire Terrier

Greyhounds

Greyhounds are typically very intelligent, tranquil, and compassionate. Greyhounds include:

Afghan Hound	Borzoi
Deerhound	Greyhound
Irish Wolfhound	Italian Greyhound
Magyar Agar	Pharaoh Hound
Saluki	Sloughi
Spanish Greyhound	Whippet

As you learned in this chapter, there are hundreds of dog breeds! And this list doesn't even include the newer crossbred dogs such as the Labradoodle and Goldendoodle. With so many wonderful dogs to choose from, you should have no trouble finding the perfect dog for you and your family—if you know what to look for.

In the next chapter, you will learn how to choose the best dog for you and your family.

Chapter 2:
Choosing a Dog

You are probably reading this E-book because you are thinking about getting a new puppy or dog, or you may have a dog already, but you just need to learn how to train it. This chapter is geared towards the person who is thinking about getting a new puppy or dog.

Your hopes are that new this addition to your family will be an exciting and paw-sitive experience! For many families, it is. But it can also be a less-than-pleasant experience for other families.

How do you make your puppy experience a great experience? It has to do with finding the right puppy for you and your family. The only way to do this is through preparation and research.

Bringing a new puppy into your household is a major change for everyone—your family and the puppy. Everyone is affected in some way. You may get less sleep because of your puppy's early wake-up call. Your spouse may have to come home during his or her lunch hour to let the puppy out. Maybe your child will need to take the puppy for a walk after school.

As tempting as it may be to rush out and buy the first puppy that you fall in love with, there are many things that you need to think about. This chapter will help you get a clear understanding of exactly why you want a puppy, things you need to consider, questions to ask yourself, and where to buy your puppy. You will even learn about what to do if you think you made the wrong choice in puppies.

Why Do You Want a Puppy?

Think about all the reasons you want a puppy. Be honest.

Do you want a puppy because:

- You live alone and want some companionship?

- You moved into a new area and want a "security system?"

- Your children have been asking for one and you want to teach them responsibility?

- You want to give another pet a playmate?

- You want a status symbol?

- You want an exercise partner?

- You want to rescue one that has been abandoned?

Are there any other reasons that you want a puppy?

These are all valid reasons for wanting a puppy—as long as you are prepared to take the responsibility of giving it a good home. However, the absolute best reason for wanting a puppy is because you and your family want to share many years of companionship that a dog can offer.

It is important to take your time when making the decision about buying a puppy. If you are reading the newspaper and see an advertisement for a puppy and decide on a whim to purchase one that day, you will be putting yourself, your household, and the puppy under a lot of unnecessary stress.

However, if you think carefully about it and research your options, you could have a wonderful puppy purchasing experience.

Things to Consider Before Buying a Puppy

There is a lot to think about before you welcome a new puppy into your home. Read about the issues below and think about your personal situation. Bringing your attention to these now will help prevent any unexpected "surprises" after you bring a new puppy into your home.

Your Lifestyle

Are you the type of person who travels a lot—either for work or pleasure? Or, you just like to get out of the house as much as possible? If are a person who enjoys being away from home rather than spending time at home, then you might not be ready to commit to a puppy yet.

However, if you don't travel very much and you enjoy spending time at your home, then your lifestyle can probably accommodate a puppy at this time.

This isn't to say that by having a puppy you can never leave your home. Of course you can! But generally speaking, if you are away at work all day, then you prefer to spend your evenings out also, it would not be fair for your puppy to spend so much time by himself.

Your Family

Do you live by yourself or do you live with a roommate, spouse, and/or children? Or, maybe you are caring for an elderly family member? How do these people feel about you bringing a puppy into the household?

Taking into consideration the other members of your household is something that shouldn't be overlooked as you are considering a puppy. If you live with others, you need to make sure that everyone agrees to welcome a puppy into the home.

Hopefully everyone will be just as enthusiastic about a new puppy as you. However, if anyone does not agree to the new addition, you need to find out the reason why. Does a young child have a fear of dogs? Is your spouse concerned about the financial obligations? There may be an easy solution to the concern, or there might not be in which case you may need to reconsider a puppy.

If you have children, handicapped, or senior citizens in your home, consider breeds that are appropriate for them.

Dogs that are generally good with children include:

Airedale Terrier	Basset Hound
Beagle	Bearded Collie
Bichon Frise	Boston Terrier
Boxer	Brussels Griffon
Bulldog	Cocker Spaniel
English Toy Spaniel	Golden Retriever
Great Dane	Irish Terrier
Japanese Chin	Labrador Retriever
Miniature Dachshund	Miniature Pinscher
Norfolk Terrier	Norwich Terrier
Shetland Sheepdog (Sheltie)	Shih Tzu
Standard Dachshund	Standard Schnauzer

Your Personality

What type of personality do you have? Do you like to be by yourself or do you enjoy the company of others? Are you cranky in the morning or do wake up full of energy? Are you shy or outgoing? Are you selfish or giving?

Your personality is a very important factor and it will affect your puppy's happiness. If you tend to be grumpy all the time and you direct that grumpiness towards your puppy, he will think that he is doing something wrong and might shy away from you. If you are generally happy, your puppy will be more responsive to you.

If you exude a personality that is compassionate, friendly, joyful, positive, energetic, humorous and patient, then you will most likely be compatible with a puppy. If you can't have a sense of humor in a puppy's silly and somewhat mischievous habits, then you might not be ready for a puppy yet.

Your Home

You want your new puppy to feel comfortable right away in your home! So think about the size, the layout, and the furnishings to help you know what type of dog would be at ease in your home.

What kind of home do you live in? Do you live in an apartment with a small amount of space? Or do you live in a house with a back yard? If you have a back yard, to you have a fence? Do you have a lot of stairs? What about the furnishings? Do you own a lot of expensive rugs and breakable items? Do you have adequate space in a nice quiet area for a crate?

You will need to not only think about the living space that you can provide your puppy, but also outside space to eliminate. If you live in an apartment, is there plenty of grass around to walk your dog? Also, are you allowed to walk your dog on this grass? Is the area well lit for nighttime strolls?
Whatever your case may be, you will most likely need to make some puppy-proofing steps to ensure your puppy's safety. You will learn about puppy-proofing later in Chapter 3.

Your Neighbors

As a responsible puppy owner, you need to think about how your puppy will affect your neighbors. After all, you would hope that they would do the same for you! If you live in an apartment, will your puppy's bark bother your neighbors? It would be a good idea to review your apartment building's pet policy before buying a puppy. Some apartments may charge fines—or worse eviction—for too many complaints made against excessive barking.

If you live in a house, do you have a fence to prevent the puppy from going into your neighbors' yards and possibly chewing up their flowers and gardens? If you do not have a fence, you will need to keep him on a leash or under close supervision when he is outside.

Your Neighborhood

You want your puppy to be safe and entertained—when you walk him around the neighborhood. Next time you are out, take a look around to see if your puppy would be comfortable going on walks.

Ask yourself questions such as: Are the sidewalks in good condition? Are the streets well- lit? Are there parks nearby? Are there nice wide walking trails in the area? Are there other dogs around your neighborhood and if so how do they usually react around each other?

Your Health

A new puppy is going to demand a lot of attention from you, so you will want to be in good shape to keep up with him! Take a good look at your health conditions. Are you in adequate health to handle a puppy? For example, are you allergic to any breeds? Do your allergies flare up when you are outside?

Are you physically capable of handling a puppy? You will need to consider your strength as the puppy grows to a full-size dog. Will you be able to lift him up and carry him if necessary?

Also consider the amount of exercise that your puppy may need. If he requires long walks at a time, are you able to accommodate him?

Your Budget

Raising a puppy is not cheap! It takes a lot of money to keep them looking good and feeling great. So are you prepared to handle the financial responsibilities that come along with raising a puppy?

Here is a sample of the types of costs you can expect:

- **The puppy** – The prices range of a new puppy varies significantly depending on whether you purchase him from an animal shelter, pet store, or breeder. The estimated cost is anywhere from no cost to up to $1500, depending on what type of breed you buy and where you buy it. Buying a dog from an animal shelter is little or no cost. Buying a common breed from a breeder is usually around $300-$500. However, breeds that are more desirable or that come from a very reputable breeder can be between $500 and $1500. If your new puppy is going to be shipped in an airplane, find out beforehand if shipping is part of the advertised cost. Some breeders charge a few extra hundred dollars for shipping.

- **Scheduled veterinarian visits** - Depending on the reason for your appointment, a visit can cost anywhere from under $50 to a few hundred (or more for operations).

- **Unexpected veterinarian visits** – Again, from under $50 to a few hundred (or more.)

- **Dog food** – Don't buy the cheapest dog food you can buy. You want to make sure your puppy receives important nutrients so ask your veterinarian what brands he or she recommends.

- **Crate** – Crates typically range anywhere from $30-$250, depending on the size and type of crate you choose.

- **Bedding** – You can find nice bedding for under $100.

- **Leash** – Leashes typically range in price anywhere from $3-$30, depending on the length and type of material.

- **Collar** – You can usually find a good selection of collars under $30. Of course, there are many fancy collars for the "diva" dog.

- **Grooming supplies** - Shampoo, brush, nail clippers, and other grooming supplies can add up. You can expect to pay between $20 or more for all the essentials.

- **Regular flea, tick, and heartworm treatments** – Your veterinarian will be able to help you find the treatments that are best for your dog. The price will depend on the brands.

- **Toys** – It is fun to buy your puppy lots of toys, but the price can really add up! Most toys are in the $3-$5 range, but some are more.

- **Treats, treats, and more treats!** – Make sure you buy treats that are appropriate for your puppies weight and age. It is good to have a nice variety on hand so he doesn't get bored. A box of treats is typically around $3-$5. There are "gourmet" treats that usually have a "gourmet" price tag to match.

Your Schedule

A new puppy is very dependent on his owners. Therefore, you will need to ensure that your regular schedule and the schedule of your family can accommodate the needs of a new puppy.

Take an honest look at your schedule and ask yourself questions such as: What kind of schedule do I have? Do I work long hours? Is my schedule flexible enough to leave work to let my puppy out? If I need to take my puppy to the veterinarian unexpectedly, am I able to?

And when you are home, are you willing to give up your "free time" to devote to training, exercising, and playing with your puppy? You will want to get into the habit of making time for your puppy.

Your Climate

What kind of climate do you live in? Do you have steamy hot summers or blistery cold winters? Do you have a lot of rain and wind?

You will need to make sure that the climate you live in is appropriate for your breed of puppy. Unfortunately, not all dogs can handle all types of climate conditions and you don't want to make going outside in the elements a miserable task for them. Otherwise, they may have more frequent accidents in the house.

A pug and other short-nosed breeds are not ideal for extreme heat, so an air conditioner would be necessary. Also, you would want to only take him out for lengthy walks in the early morning or late evenings.

Additionally, many small toy dogs such as those that are delicate with short hair are not ideal for extreme cold weather. Other dogs that may be larger, may not like rain and wind.

More Questions to Ask Yourself Before Getting a Puppy

As you are realizing by now, there are a lot of questions to ask yourself in regards to getting a puppy. This is a very important exercise for you be confident that you are making the right decision for you and your family. Below are some more questions for you to ask.

Will my living situation change soon?

Are you currently living by yourself and planning to get married soon? Are you about to add a baby to your family? Will a roommate be moving out in the near future?

These are all valid questions. If you will be getting married soon, is your future spouse in support of a new puppy? If you are bringing a new baby into your house, are you prepared for so many changes at once? And if a roommate will be moving out soon, are you willing to handle all the responsibilities by yourself?

Will I be moving anytime soon?

You may have a good home for a new puppy now, but are you planning to move anytime soon? If so, do you know what type of home you'll be moving into and is it a dog-friendly area? If you are moving into a house, is the yard fenced-in? If you are moving into an apartment, will it allow pets?

What size of dog do I want?

You may already know the size of dog you want—small, medium, or large. But there are a few things to consider before you make the purchase. If you live in an apartment or you rent a house, there are probably size restrictions to the pets you can keep—if you can keep them at all.

Very small dogs can generally get most of their physical exercise requirements in a house, or even a small apartment. Larger dogs need more floor space to move about and usually require outdoor exercise as well.

Smaller dogs usually can perform training exercises indoors, whereas larger dogs may need more space—either indoors or outdoors. If you are concerned about letting your dog outside to eliminate, small dogs can usually be trained to go inside the house on papers or a mat. However, larger dogs produce a greater amount of waste, so this can be difficult to manage, especially if you are gone for long periods of time.

Smaller dogs typically have a longer life span than larger dogs. It is not uncommon for a smaller dog to live a healthy 14 years, where a larger dog may live to only be around 10 years old. Of course, the quality of life that you provide him can impact the length of his life.

Smaller dogs usually create less destruction during the puppy chewing stage than larger dogs with bigger teeth and stronger jaws.

All puppies start out small, just make sure you know how big it will grow up to be and provide some "wiggle room." For example, if you think you are purchasing a miniature long-haired dachshund, don't be surprised if it is actually a cross between a "miniature" and a "standard."

What personality of dog do I want?

With every dog comes a different personality! Some are sweet and cuddly. Some are lively and energetic. Some are more playful than others. Some are humorous while others are not easily amused. Some just love the sound of their bark and others are more reserved.
To ensure that your dog will be a "best friend" research the different breeds to find a personality that will compliment yours.

How much time am I willing to exercise the puppy?

If you are the type of person who does not like to go for long walks now, getting a dog probably won't change your mind about walking. Think about the time you have available and the level of exercise you are willing to endure for your dog.

Dogs that require little exercise (for example, occasional walks) include:

- Affenpinscher
- Bichon Frise
- Chihuahua
- English Toy Spaniel
- Japanese Chin
- Maltese
- Miniature Dachshund
- Papillon
- Shih Tzu
- Toy Poodle

The above mentioned dogs also enjoy plenty of indoor play time. A walk outside is a real treat, so you will want to make the effort for walks at least a couple times a week.

Dogs that require a moderate level of exercise (for example, walks five or six days a week for about 10 to 20 minutes) include:

- Brussels Griffon
- Cairn Terrier
- Italian Greyhound
- Miniature Pinscher
- Miniature Poodle
- Miniature Schnauzer
- Norfolk Terrier
- Norwich Terrier
- Toy Fox Terrier
- Toy Manchester Terrier

The above mentioned dogs also enjoy lots of indoor play session. These types of dogs enjoy both short walks and longer walks.

Dogs that require medium level of exercise (for example walks five or six days a week ranging from 15 to 30 minutes) include:

- Basenji
- Basset Hound
- Beagle
- Boston Terrier
- Bulldog
- Cardigan Welsh Corgi
- Cocker Spaniel
- Shetland Sheepdog (Sheltie)
- Standard Dachshund
- Standard Poodle

Along with their walks, the above mentioned dogs should enjoy indoor play sessions daily. All of the dogs would be excited for longer walks, except for the bulldog. You could also do two smaller walks rather than one long walk.

Dog's that require a high level of exercise (for example brisk walks five or six days a week for 20 to 90 minutes) include:

- Airedale Terrier
- Bearded Collie
- Boxer
- Dalmation
- Golden Retriever
- Great Dane
- Irish Terrier
- Labrador Retriever
- Standard Schnauzer
- Whippet

The length of walk really depends on the dog's energy level. It may be easier to break down the walks into shorter time segments.

Also, the above mentioned dogs tend to love runs, so if an open-fenced in area is available, treat him to some running time. If, on occasion, you can't spend a lot of time outside due to the weather, make sure the dog receives a lot of indoor play time.

How much time am I willing to groom the puppy?

Grooming takes time and effort, so you will need to think about how much time (and patience) you can dedicate to grooming your pooch. Of course, if you don't want to do the grooming yourself, you can take your puppy to a professional groomer.
Some breeds that are easy to groom include:

Affenpinscher,	Basenji
Basset Hound	Beagle
Boston Terrier	Boxer
Brussels Griffon	Bulldog
Cairn Terrier	Cardian Welsh Corgi
Chihuahua	Dalmatian
Golden Retriever	Great Dane
Italian Greyhound	Japanese Chin
Labrador Retriever	Miniature Schnauzer
Norfolk Terrier	Norwich Terrier
Papillon	Standard Dachshund
Toy Fox Terrier	Toy Manchester Terrier
Whippe	

What breed should I get?

Answering the questions above will help you determine the best breed for you and your family. The main thing is to not only consider a breed that is good for you now, but several years from now too.

The best thing you can do to find a breed for you is to do lots of thorough research. The positive thing about selecting a purebred dog, as compared to a mixed breed, is that you can better predict their size, temperament, coat, health concerns, and grooming requirements. When you know what type of dog your puppy will grow up to be, you can better anticipate what types of preparations you will need to make.

Where to Buy Your Puppy?

There are several options available to you for buying your puppy, including animal shelters, pet stores, and breeders. Below is a description of each.

An Animal Shelter

If you are looking for the cheapest option for buying a puppy, adopting one from an animal shelter would be your best bet. The cost is actually very minimal. Additionally, when you buy your dog from an animal shelter, you are often eligible for a reduced rate on spaying and neutering.

Another benefit from getting your dog from your local animal shelter is that you will be saving the life of a dog that if not claimed or adopted, would otherwise be put to sleep. There is an enormous population of dogs that are sent to these shelters, and if you adopt from these you are helping to control this ever-growing pet population.

Animal shelters usually have a wide selection of mixed breeds. Usually less than half are actually purebreds. But just because there isn't a big selection of purebreds does not mean that you can't find a wonderful pet. Just be sure to try to find out as much about his background as possible from the animal shelter. For rescued dogs that were strayed, this information is usually very limited.

There are many reasons why dogs end up in the shelter. Some dogs end up there because the owners didn't want them any more. Maybe the dog misbehaved and the owners couldn't properly train him. Maybe the owner was getting too old to take care of the dog. Or maybe the family was moving to a home that didn't accept dogs. Another common reason for dogs being sent to the shelter is because they ran away and didn't have an identification tag. In this case, hopefully the owners will come back to rescue their dog.

If you spend some time talking with the staff about your questions and concerns about adopting from an animal shelter, they should be able to help you determine which dogs are best for your family.

When you are looking at a dog at an animal shelter, spend time playing with him. Take notice of how responsive he is to you. Does he perk up and wag his tail in excitement? Or, is he very shy and meek? Does he look healthy? Are there any known health conditions that he has? Do you know what breed(s) he is?

A Pet Store

Buying a dog from a pet store is certainly convenient. These stores usually have a nice selection of cute dogs to choose from.

Owners of pet stores will tell you that a benefit from buying a dog from a pet store is that the dog has had an opportunity to be sociable with all the people that come through including employees, customers, and window shoppers.
However, some pet stores have become the target of criticism for alleged inhumane treatment of their animals. For example, they may not get all of the medical attention they need. Or, they may have highly infectious diseases. Or, they may be kept in cages that are just too small for them.

Oftentimes, the dogs that you see in the pet stores are actually purchased from puppy mills. These are unethical breeders who breed dogs in mass quantity for profit only.

Dogs produced in puppy mills usually live in filthy conditions, with no regard for improving the quality of the breed. These puppies are usually sick, underfed, dirty, and have been mistreated. These dogs are generally reproduced with each other, passing on grave genetic defects for many generations. Some people think that if you buy a puppy from a puppy store, you are actually supporting the operation of puppy mills.

If you want to buy a puppy from a pet store, make sure it is a reliable store by asking some questions and handling the dogs. Does the dog look healthy? Check his weight, eyes, ears, coat, etc.

Ask if the pet store can provide you with references of owners who have previously purchased dogs from the store. If they really care about the puppies and the homes they go into, they will probably have this information for you.

Another clue to determine if a pet store is reputable is by the number of questions they ask you. If the staff is truly concerned about the future of the dog, they will want to know about your lifestyle and living condition, too.

A Reputable Breeder

There are many advantages to buying a puppy from a breeder. In fact, buying a puppy from a reputable breeder is the preferred—and safest—way to buy a puppy. Once you select on a breed (or breeds), try to find the most reputable and experienced breeders you can.

A reputable breeder is one that truly cares about the quality of the breed more so than making fast money. A reputable breeder is very selective about what dogs are bred together. Their goal is to continually improve the quality of the dogs they produce. This includes physical traits as well as temperament.

Buying from a reputable breeder is the best way you can find out about the dog's background. In many cases, you can ask for documents verifying that a particular line of dogs is free of conditions, if any that affect certain breeds. Don't be surprised if you can't find a reputable breeder for the breed(s) you want in your city. Some people search out of state, out of region, or even out of country to find the right breeder. But it is worth the search to know that you have a high-quality puppy that has been breed with the utmost care.

It is best to meet with a breeder before you want to purchase a puppy. (If you do, leave your money at home so you don't spontaneously decide to buy one on the spot!) At the very minimum, have a phone call conversation with the breeder. You will see a section below titled **"Questions to Ask a Breeder"** to learn what questions you should ask your prospective breeder.

When you meet with the breeder, ask to meet the puppy's parents. If you are truly dealing with a reputable breeder, they will have no hesitation with you meeting the parents. Meeting the sire and dam will give you a good idea of what your puppy will probably look like when it is full grown.

Pay attention to the parents' physical characteristics and temperament. Are they alert and playful? Do they appear healthy and happy? Would you feel comfortable living with these dogs? Also look around to see what kind of conditions the puppy is living in. Is the breeder's home clean? Is the puppy's sleeping area clean and comfortable?

The best breeders will also extensively question prospective dog owners about their lifestyles and living situations. In fact, you should feel like you are being interviewed just as you are interviewing the breeder. The breeder should ask you all sorts of questions about your lifestyle, your family, your home, your knowledge of raising puppies, etc. Although rarely done, you should not be surprised if a breeder asks to see your home.

The only downside to buying from a reputable breeder is the cost. Breeders do charge a lot, especially if the puppy is from a high-quality bloodline. However, if you want a puppy that you can be confident of his temperament, appearance, etc., buying from a breeder is absolutely the best option.

This is particularly true if, for example, someone in your family has allergies and can only live with a certain coat type. If you buy a dog from a pet store or an animal shelter, you take a risk of not knowing for certain. Of course, the cost of the puppy depends on the breed and the breeder's reputation. A breeder with a strong reputation can get by charging more.

If you do not know of any reputable breeders, you can ask around to local humane societies, veterinarian offices, friends, etc. There are a lot of good breeder websites too.

Amateur Breeder

An amateur breeder is one that is not a professional, but rather someone who might be a neighbor or friend whose dog has been bred. In this situation, the dogs probably were not selectively bred for appearance and temperament as a professional breeder would have done.

However, if the puppy was produced by two great dogs, you will most likely get a great dog too. A lot of families find an excellent dog this way and it is typically not as expensive as buying from a professional breeder.

This amateur breeder will most likely be able to provide you with some information about the puppy. At least, more information than you would know from an animal shelter or pet store.

A Non-Reputable Breeder

A non-reputable breeder is anyone who does not have the intentions of improving the quality of life for a particular breed. This is a breeder who is only concerned with producing mass quantities of puppies and selling them. This type of breeder does not care about the puppy's living conditions or who it will go home with.

This type of breeder could very likely be running a puppy mill. Stay away from this type of breeder!

Questions to Ask a Breeder

When you speak with a breeder, either on the phone or in person, have a list in front of you containing all of the questions you want to ask. It is better to ask too many questions, than not enough.

Questions for the breeder:

- How long have you been breeding puppies?

- What can you tell me about the breed?

- Why are you selling the puppy?

- What health testing has been done for the puppy?

- Has the puppy received his first vaccination?

- Has he been desexed?

- What kind of socialization has the puppy received?

- How did he react to the socialization?

- Does anything seem to frighten the puppy?

- What has the puppy been eating so far?

- How often do you feed him?

- Are the parents registered with any organizations?

- Do you have references of previous customers that I can contact?

- What policies do you have if the puppy turns out to be sick or defected?

- Can I contact you if I have any future questions?

Physical Check

Whether you decide on a puppy from an animal shelter, a pet store, or a breeder, you need to examine him from head to toe. There may be some obvious clues as to the health condition of the puppy.

Look closely into the pup's eyes to make sure that they are nice and clear. Open his mouth to see that the gums are pink and healthy. Gently rub his belly and look for protrusions. This would indicate that he might have a hernia. If his tummy is bloated, he may have worms.

Take notice of the puppy's stance. Do all four legs look properly aligned? Does he walk with a limp or look like he's in discomfort?

You will also want to check his vision and hearing. How does the puppy respond to your movements? Do his eyes follow you? How does the puppy respond to your voice? Try clapping your hands? How does he react?

So what happens if you find what seems to be the perfect puppy, yet there seems to be minor health concerns? For example, maybe he has ear mites. This happens to be a common ailment that can be treated by a veterinarian.

If the puppy has a health concern that you are just not sure about, request that the puppy be examined by a veterinarian before you buy the puppy. Many places that sell dogs will allow a veterinary examination within the first one or two weeks of purchase. If a major problem is found, a full refund may be given.

If you are buying from a reputable breeder, he or she has most likely already had the puppy examined with its appropriate shots given. (Another great reason to buy from a puppy from a reputable breeder!) Be sure that you fully understand the return policy before you purchase the puppy. Of course, within a couple days after you purchase your puppy you should take him to a veterinarian for a thorough check-up.

What if You Made the Wrong Choice?

What happens if you purchase a puppy that you and your family are really excited about, but once you have him home for awhile, you realize that it isn't a good match?

Maybe raising a puppy is more responsibility than you anticipated. Maybe your dog's temperament isn't what you expected it to be. Or maybe there is a major change in your life that disables you from giving the dog the attention it needs.

If you realize that you made the wrong choice purchasing a puppy, the best thing you can do is to be proactive in finding him a new home. This should be done right away. The longer you keep the dog with your family, the more difficult it will be for the dog to adjust to another new home.

If you purchased the dog from a breeder, you can call him or her to ask if you could return it. They may or may not take it back. If they do, you shouldn't expect to get all your money back, although if you do, that is great. If the breeder will not take back your dog, or if you did not originally purchase the dog from a breeder, contact your local human society for a list of organizations that might be able to help you find an owner. You can also inquire with individual businesses about placing flyers in their lobbies such as veterinary offices, pet stores, grocery stores, etc. Another option is to place newspaper ads and even ads on websites.

In the meantime, it is important for you to make every effort to keep your puppy happy and healthy while you try to find him a new home.

Choosing a dog is a big decision. As you learned in Chapter 2, there are many different considerations for choosing the best one for you and your family.

Once you find the perfect dog for you and your family, you will learn how to bring the new puppy or dog into your home. This topic is covered next in Chapter 3.

Chapter 3:
Bringing Your Puppy Home

So you've found the perfect puppy for you and your family, congratulations! Now, you have to think about preparing for his big arrival. This includes the car ride home, puppy-proofing your home, setting up his space, and setting the expectations for everyone in your family.

Taking the time to prepare for your puppy's arrival is important. The more preparation you make before he comes home, the less stressful it will be for everyone when he arrives home.

Picture this scenario: You arrive home with your puppy and you are scrambling to put away anything that your puppy could get into and destroy. You are carrying his bulky crate from the laundry room to the kitchen to the family room trying to find the perfect spot for it. You are ignoring your puppy as you are frantically trying to get everything just right.

Is that a very compassionate welcome for your puppy? Of course it isn't. Instead, figure out all of these details before his arrival and he will feel like you really want him to be "part of the pact."

This chapter is focused on bringing a new puppy home, but the same concepts can apply for bringing home an older dog too.

Caution: The first few days could be a little nerve-wracking, but as long as you prepare, you and your family can welcome your puppy home with open paws!

When to Bring Your Puppy Home

Once you have your heart set on a puppy, you will be tempted to bring him home as soon as you possibly can. Try not to get too anxious though. Instead, be patient. You want to make sure that your puppy—and your home—is in excellent condition for the new arrival!

The Appropriate Age

It is recommended that a new puppy should not be removed from his mother until the age range of 7 to 12 weeks of age. Some reputable breeders insist on waiting until after 8 weeks of age.

Yes, you will oftentimes see newspaper or web-site ads that offer puppies for sale at the young age of 6 weeks (or even younger), but purchase at that age is highly discouraged. It is ok to pay a deposit at that time, but you should not take the puppy from his mother yet.

The Appropriate Time

Think carefully of the best time to bring home a new puppy. For example, if everyone in your household is at work or school all day, it would not be a good idea to bring the pup home during the week when everyone is busy.

If there is a long holiday week approaching when everyone (or at least some people) will be home, try to schedule the puppy's arrival during that time. This way, not only will you have plenty of time to help the puppy adjust, but you will have some back-up support as well.

If a week-long holiday week is not in your near future, consider the next best option—a three-day holiday weekend. If this is not possible anytime soon either, you should try for a weekend. You may wish to schedule an extra day or two off of work just to give yourself more time.

It is best that during the first few days you have a new puppy home that someone— whether you or another family member—is around at all times. After the puppy has had a chance to settle in, then you can more comfortably leave him home alone.

If all of this concern with time seems to be a bit overboard to you, just remember that this transfer of homes is one of the most important milestones in your puppy's life. Helping your puppy adjust to your home with plenty of care and compassion will make it a better, more positive experience for everyone!

Find a Veterinarian

You should actually try and find a veterinarian before you bring your puppy home. You may already be familiar with excellent veterinarians in your area, but if you are not check around.

Ask friends and neighbors who they use. You can even stop by different veterinary offices to get a feel for the place. Look for such things as cleanliness of the facility, friendliness of the staff, customers' expressions, awards on the walls, informational flyers, etc.

If a veterinary office doesn't have very much activity going on (for example, not many customers around) there might be a good reason why. If there is too much activity going on, that might mean the office is understaffed and you might not get a veterinary's full attention.

Puppy Preparations

So how ready is your home—inside and out—for a new puppy? Make sure you have a day (or more) marked on your calendar for making all the necessary preparations.

It is not a challenging task, but rather a proactive exercise that not only prevents your valuables from being destroyed, but also protects the health and safety of the puppy. The best rule of thumb is to just use common sense.

If you have raised a puppy before, you probably have a pretty good idea of the types of precautions you need to take. Below are some helpful tips to help you prepare for puppy's big "move in" day!

Puppy Proofing Your Home

Walk through your home room by room and take notice of things that might be within your puppy's reach—and curiosity! Oh yes, you know that beautiful plant that is nicely perched on the coffee table? Is that something that your puppy will be able to get his paws on easily? If so, you better find a new spot for it or you could be in for a messy surprise when you least expect it.

What about electrical cords and drapery cords? What seem like non-interesting objects to us, are fun and interesting chewing objects for your puppy!
Magazine racks and low book shelves are another open invitation for puppies. They love to chew paper!

How about shoes on shoe racks, clothes in clothes baskets, and clothes folded on low closet shelves? If you don't want to see your shoes and unmentionables dragged around the house, it would be a good idea to keep these high out of reach, or keep your closet door closed. Does your kitchen have low cupboards or counters with tempting food items inside? If so, keep the food well-concealed or move to higher cupboards. Also, be sure that detergents and any cleaning supplies are out of his reach. These cleaners can be toxic if he would happen to consume them.

Your bathroom is another place of unusual objects—prescription bottles, over-the-counter medications, cosmetics, dental care, soaps, shampoo, razors, etc. Keep everything out of puppy's reach.

If consumed, these products could be severely dangerous to your puppy. Watch out for choking hazards too, such as caps off of medication bottles, tubes of toothpaste, etc.

You may have children who are excited about getting a new puppy, but unless they want to share their favorite toys with the pooch, they should keep them out of his reach and view.

Puppy Proofing Your Yard

If you live in a house, your puppy will probably be spending a lot of time outdoors. Unless your yard is fenced in you should keep your puppy on a leash until you are completely confident that he will come to you when you give the "come" command. (You will learn this command in Chapter 10.)

If you don't have a traditional fence, you could think about using an invisible or wireless fence. These "correct" the puppy from wandering to far. These are a cheaper alternative to a real fence, and although they are effective, there is no 100% guarantee that they will work perfectly every time.

Some plants can be dangerous for your puppy so if you have plants, flowers, or gardens in your yard, you will want to take measures to isolate and protect them.
Make sure your yard is clear of any debris, glass, or objects that he could choke on. Also, if you have gardening tools and sprays, keep them out of reach as well.

Puppy Proofing Your Garage

It is not recommended that your puppy spend much time in the garage. However, he will most likely walk through it to get to the car for his fun car rides!

Take a close look for any sharp tools that may be lying around. Lawnmowers, weed eaters, snow blowers, and electrical tools can all be very dangerous as well. If you need to, invest in shelves or racks to keep your garage supplies up high and out of your puppy's reach.

Set Schedules

If you live with a spouse, children, or a roommate, and they plan to help you take care of the puppy, you should create a schedule for everyone to follow. Post this on the refrigerator or other high-traffic area.

The schedule should include activities such as when to take the puppy out, when to walk him, when to play with him, when to feed him, when to bathe him, when to brush him, etc.

If this schedule is determined and agreed upon before the puppy arrives home, there will be less confusion and less chance of someone forgetting an important responsibility.

Setting up Space for Puppy

Just as everyone in your home has their own space, your puppy should have his own space too. Even the smallest toy dogs—who don't take up much physical space—need their own quiet space.

Selecting a Crate

Giving your puppy his own space with a crate will make him feel safe and secure—like a den. This dedicated space also helps to keep your puppy from having accidents and destruction through chewing.

When you buy a crate for your puppy, you want to find one that is big enough for your puppy to stand up in and turn around comfortably. Anything smaller will be too restrictive for him.

Anything larger might encourage him to sleep in one area and eliminate in another.

Common crate sizes are:

- *20" W x 24" D x 21" H*

- *23" W x 36" D x 24" H*

- *25" W x 31.5" D x 24" H*

- *30" W x 48" D x 36" H*

- *47" W x 57" D x 45" H*

If you don't want to buy a larger crate as your puppy grows to full size, you can simply buy a larger crate from the beginning and then add a panel to block off part of it. This way, as he grows you can adjust the panel.

There are two types of crates available: plastic and metal. Both are acceptable and both have different benefits. The plastic crate is lighter in weight so it is easier to move around your home and it is easier for traveling. A plastic crate generally is more enclosed.

A metal crate is usually more durable so they tend to have a longer lifespan. Metal crates also offer more ventilation. During nighttime when your puppy is sleeping, you may want to cover part of the metal crate with a blanket so he can sleep better.

Placement of the Crate

During the day, it is beneficial for you to keep the crate in an area of the house where there is family activity such as the kitchen or family room. Placing the crate in a laundry room, basement, or other distant room will make your puppy feel isolated from the rest of the family.

During the night when your puppy is sleeping in his crate, it is a good idea for you to keep it in your bedroom. This will not only make him feel like he wasn't abandoned, but it will also allow you to hear him when he cries to go outside.

If you prefer not to keep the crate in your bedroom while you are sleeping, try to keep it in a room near the outside door. That way, when you go to let him out, he will not have far to walk to go outside to eliminate.

Crate Accessories

Certainly, you want your puppy to feel right at home in his crate! Therefore, you should make sure that it is fully-equipped with a bed and toys.

You want your puppy to have access to water while he is in his crate, but you don't want to provide too much because he might not be able to hold it all until he is let out. A small hamster water bottle generally provides enough water for shorter periods of time spent in a crate. It is also not advised to keep food in the crate. However, a few treats are always encouraged!

The Ride Home

The car ride home could be a scary experience for your little puppy. If you will be driving through big cities with heavy traffic, he could be in for a surprise.

Next time you are in your car, take notice of all the strange sounds: honking horns, emergency vehicle sirens, dogs barking, road construction noises, loud music, cars backfiring, etc.

A dog's hearing is extremely developed. He will be able to hear sounds that we cannot. So what you may think is a "normal" ride through the city, could be quite traumatic for the puppy.

If you are driving your puppy home, keep him safe and secure in a padded box or traveling case. Or, if another family member is with you, he or she can hold the puppy in their lap. Either way, make sure he receives plenty of love pats and soothing words of comfort during the drive.

Of course, you are always a safe driver, but when you are driving with your puppy for the first time, it is wise to be extra cautious. Drive carefully, don't step on the brake to quickly, and don't take turns to sharply.

This will most likely be your puppy's first or second car ride, so you want to make sure it is a pleasant experience for him. Offer him a few treats during the ride. Be sure to bring along some old towels or blankets, just in case all of this excitement causes him to have an accident. If it is long ride, he will most likely sleep part of the way.

Introducing Puppy to the Family

When you pull up to your home, you will probably want to let your puppy eliminate outside before bringing him inside. After he takes care of business, bring him into the house very gently and talk to him in the same soothing manner that you did during the car ride.

Talk with your family beforehand about how to greet the new puppy. Introductions should be done in a very calm and loving way. It is hard, especially for young children, to remain calm upon meeting their puppy for the first time, but it is essential. Too much excitement can scare the puppy.

Each family member should take the opportunity to gently pet and speak with the puppy individually. Too many hands on the puppy at the same time could frighten him. Encourage each family member to give him a yummy treat so he knows that everyone is friendly.

As your family spends more time with the puppy, make sure your children know a few key rules. They should know how to gently stroke the puppy in nice long sweeps. They should know to put the puppy up with both hands, one under the chest between the front two legs, and the other one supporting the puppy's rear end. Also, children should never tease or disturb the puppy when he is eating or resting.

Be aware that your puppy is going to be very nervous and shy during this introduction time. That is perfectly natural. After all, this is a new home and a new pack, so he is not quite sure what to expect.

Introducing Puppy to Other Pets

If you have other pets in your home, you will need to introduce your puppy with care. Getting off on the wrong "paw" can be dangerous for your new puppy that could cause many problems down the road!

If you have more than one other pet, introduce your new puppy to each one individually. Calmly bring the two pets together, each being held by a separate person in a neutral territory. For example, don't introduce your puppy next to an older dog's food bowl or bed. Outside in the yard or an open room such as a family room is a good option for the introductions. Some experts recommend introducing them through a crate.

Let them have an opportunity to sniff each other and talk to them in a pleasant and positive tone, giving them lots of treats. You want your pets to know that bringing the new puppy into the home is a good thing. Once they have had a chance to get to know each other, separate them so neither has a chance to get aggressive. Make sure you give your older dog plenty of attention—just as much as the puppy.

Make sure you give your new puppy his own food and water bowls, crate, bed, and toys. This way your older dog will not feel like anything is being taken away from him.

For several days after your puppy's new arrival, give the pets plenty of opportunities for controlled playtime. This playtime, and any time that they the pets are spending time together, should always be supervised.

It may take several weeks or even months before the pets can be trusted to play together nicely and unsupervised. But until then, it is absolutely critical that they are supervised to ensure that aggressive behavior does not break out—and rewarding them continually when they are playing nicely together.

Don't be surprised if they don't play together right away and resist the urge of forcing them to play. It will take them some time to get used to each other, but once they do, they have the potential of being terrific play mates!

Introducing Puppy to His Crate

After the introductions, take your puppy to his new "home within the home"—his crate. Toss some treats and toys inside. Slowly guide him into his crate. He will probably sniff around and eat his treats.

When he enters, be sure to praise him with "good dog," "good boy," or "yes." Whenever he goes in or near his crate you want to praise him. However, you don't want to make a big deal when he exits his crate, or else he'll think that being outside of his crate is better than being inside his crate.

You will learn more about crate training in Chapter 9.

A Trip to the Veterinarian

By now, you should already have your veterinarian appointment scheduled for the first day or two after you bring your puppy home and after he has had a chance to settle in.

During this time, your puppy will be checked over thoroughly and given any necessary shots. Until your puppy has had all of his shots, your veterinarian may recommend that you not take him for walks outside. This is a protective measure against contracting infectious diseases.

In this chapter, you learned about how to make preparations for bringing home your puppy. You will be thankful that you did all this work before your puppy's arrival. That way, you can enjoy your new family member and not worry about running around making last-minute preparations.

In Chapter 4 you will learn how to condition your puppy to his new home.

Chapter 4:
Conditioning Your Puppy

When you bring a new puppy into your home, he is entering a whole new way of life. He is accustomed to living closely with his mother and littermates. As a tiny pup, he didn't have to worry about any "rules," he was just trying to keep warm, eat food, and learn how to be a puppy.

Now, he is living in a new home with a new family and new rules. He doesn't understand why there was a transition. It is your responsibility to give your new puppy a home that he feels safe in, food that will maintain his health, and lots of love and attention. Additionally, you will need to condition the puppy to his new world.

In this chapter you will learn how to condition your puppy in his earliest days of living with you in your home. When you take the time right away to condition him to new sights, sounds, and situations, he will grow up to be less frightful of certain situations in the future.

Your puppy will soon learn that you and your family are non-threatening. By all of the attention, love, food, and treats you give him, he will no doubt know that you are welcoming him as part of the pack. However, there are a lot of other activities that can go on inside and outside of the house that may be confusing and even scary for the puppy. These incidents could be quite traumatic for the puppy, causing fear that will make him want to always avoid the situation.

Conditioning inside the Home

A whirlwind of activities go on—day in and day out—in your home. Everyone is busy and has their own activities from taking care of the house, to doing homework, to cooking meals, to getting ready in the morning, to watching television.

From your puppy's perspective, all of this activity probably seems like a mass of confusion! You and your family will need to condition him to the regular activities so he can see all of this as normal. Below are some of the more frightening activities that happen inside the home.

Cleaning Day

Cleaning day can be quite a series of shocking events for a puppy. For example, let's say you take out your feather duster and you dust all of the furniture and knick knacks as you normally would. You may even jokingly dust your puppy by rubbing the duster lightly over his head!

Your puppy will most likely follow you around curiously watching the duster as it goes up and down and all around! Because you probably take pauses to pet him or say kind words to him, your puppy probably thinks you are playing with him so he may even try to catch this feathered friend! After you are done dusting, you take out the broom out of the closet and start sweeping the kitchen floor. Being brand new to the household, your puppy has never seen the broom before.

Your puppy is once again curious and closely watches your every stroke. He will try to get close to it, and oops! You accidentally bump him with the broom. He jumps back and appears frightened.

Of course, you didn't hit him intentionally, and the stroke was light enough that it doesn't hurt. But the experience itself was scary. The shock of being hit is what frightened him the most.

Next, it's time to bring out the vacuum cleaner. Still shaken, the puppy sees this monstrous object come out of the dark closet. Then, with a flip of the switch, it roars throughout the house.

This sound is terrifying to him so he'll probably run off to the corner and crouch. Meanwhile, you are vacuuming the house, room by room, not realizing the trauma your puppy is going through. So, depending on what development stage your puppy is currently in, anytime your puppy hears this sound in the future he could associate the vacuum with that terrible feeling of fear.

How do you condition your puppy to adjust to such household activities? Obviously, you can't avoid cleaning your house! And you may not even realize that your puppy has been traumatized.

First, you need to look at everything from his perspective. How do you anticipate that your puppy will react to such sights, sounds, and situations?

Second, take measures to help him adjust. For example, for something as significant as a vacuum cleaner, try starting it away from your puppy. This way, he will be able to hear it from a distance and approach it at his level of comfort. If he seems frightened, invite him to come closer.

Other Activities

Certainly, there are other incidents that go on within the house everyday that affect your puppy. For example, the sound of blenders, washing machines, musical instruments, stereos, etc.

The sites of a birthday party, a family game of charades, someone packing a suitcase, etc. Then, there will plenty of activities that directly do affect your puppy such as bathing, nail clipping, and brushing.

The key to introducing these new sights, sounds, and activities to your puppy is to do it gradually and calmly. Do what you can to make it a positive experience. Your puppy wants to please you so when he responds positively, praise him with lots of love and attention.

Conditioning for House Visitors

Most likely, people visit your home several times a week. Whether your visitors are friends, relatives, service providers, or pizza deliverers, your puppy won't know the difference.

Let's say two teenage boy neighbors come over selling candy bars for a football team fundraising event. They are both very nice boys, but being football players, they are both big and a little rowdy.

They see the new puppy and both reach down to pat him and play with him. Your puppy is shocked! Who are these people and why are they grabbing at me?
Of course, the teenage boys didn't mean any harm. They were just excited to see the little puppy and wanted to do what boys do—play! However, this isolated incident could cause a severe impact on how your puppy reacts to all future visitors.

To prevent this traumatic event from happening again, you will need to be proactive in helping your visitors know how to respond to the new puppy. As a guest arrives, you want to tell him or her at the door that you have a new puppy. Ask your guest to stay calm and not approach the puppy.

Rather, let the puppy approach the guest. The guest can certainly squat down to his level and reach out his hand slowly. This will invite the puppy to approach him more comfortably. He will sniff at the guest's hands and realize that he does not want to hurt him.

You will learn more about specific training throughout this E-book.

Conditioning Outside of the Home

A puppy not only needs conditioning inside the house—but outside as well. Think about all the unusual sights, sounds, and smells of the great outdoors! Conditioning your puppy will help him feel comfortable whether he is outside to eliminate, to play, or to go for a walk.

Outside, your puppy will be exposed to different surfaces such as grass, pavement, sand, and gravel. He will see people of all sizes, shapes, and ages when he is out for walks. He will see other animals. And he will be exposed to all the activities that go on in a town or city.

The Leash

Shortly after you bring your puppy home you should start walking him on a leash. He is going to want to do plenty of exploring outside and if your back yard doesn't have a fence, you will need a leash. And even if you do have a leash, you will want to walk him around the neighborhood to condition him for the outdoors.

It is important that you have your veterinarian's approval before walking him outside where other dogs may have eliminated. If your puppy hasn't had all his shots, he could be exposed to infectious diseases.

It may be a little awkward for at first for your puppy to walk on a leash, but he will get the hang of it. The quicker your puppy learns how to walk on a leash, the more pleasant your walks will be.

Your puppy will probably be inclined to pull on the leash. Your natural reaction will be to yank on the leash to pull him back. This, however, will only make your puppy want to pull you harder! You will learn more about training your puppy to walk nicely on a leash in later chapters.

Going for a Walk

First, you want to allow your puppy to practice walking on the leash around the backyard. Make sure that you use a long leash so he will feel free to move about as he needs to. That freedom will keep him calm and help him feel self-assured. It may take a day or two (or longer) for him to walk on it without being distracted by it. Then, once he is comfortable, you can start taking him for short walks around the neighborhood. This is a big milestone for your puppy! He will be excited and probably a little scared.

It will be your job to give him lots of encouragement and praise along the way. Until you have a chance to properly train him to walk on a leash, he will probably be walking all around you—so watch your step!

Your puppy will most definitely see unusual objects and hear strange noises during your outdoor venture. He could even show fear if he is startled by something. Imagine the sounds of wind howling, garbage cans rattling, cars honking, children yelling, airplanes flying above, fallen leaves crackling, etc.

Let's say there is an empty soda can on the sidewalk. Your puppy may stumble upon on it and jump in shock. Gently walk up to the can yourself and examine it slowly and carefully.

Then, encourage and praise your puppy. He will see that you accept the situation and the puppy will follow you to it. He will then sniff around the can and examine it thoroughly. Continue to praise him.

Once the puppy is through with the can, step back several feet and then approach the object once again, praising him. He will almost always show no suspicion as he passes the can a second time.

When you are walking your puppy, try to stay away from high-traffic areas as you are conditioning him. Imagine from your puppy's perspective what it must be like for him to look up at big, loud cars and trucks!

Start by walking him around a nice residential neighborhood or walking trail. After he is very comfortable, then you can gradually introduce him to more traffic.

Meeting People during Your Walk

Of course, you and your puppy are going to meet lots of other people on your walks! After all, who can resist saying "hi" to a cute puppy?

People will stop you and ask typical questions such as "What's his name?" "What kind of dog is he?" and "How old is he?"

This is a great opportunity for your puppy to socialize with other people. Invite your puppy up to the people and praise him. Encourage the people to extend their hands and let the puppy sniff them. Once he has accepted them, encourage the people to pet him gently.

Meeting Dogs during Your Walk

You are sure to find other dog owners out walking their dogs too! When you approach another dog—whether on leash or stray—be sure not to tug on the leash. However, you want to keep a tight grip on the leash in case he wants to dart off.

As your puppy is meeting a new dog, speak in a very calm voice with praising words.

This will be comforting to both your puppy and the other dog.

The two dogs will probably walk around each other. You will need to walk around too so that the other dog stays on the opposite side and does not get between you and your dog.

You don't want this to happen because you want to be in a good position to pull your puppy back in case a fight would break out. Also, your puppy (when he is mature) might be inclined to protect you.

When your puppy meets another dog, you should refrain from petting either one of them. If you pet the other dog, your puppy may become jealous. If you pet yours, he may become protective of you.

Also, you should never raise your voice because this may alarm the dogs. And do not bend down over your dog because this promotes protective aggression. (You will learn about protective aggression in Chapter 5.)

Your puppy will soon be conditioned to the outdoors so you can both enjoy a lovely walk together.

Conditioning your puppy to new sites, sounds, and situations is a necessary for the transition of moving into a new home. Without conditioning, more disciplined training will be a real challenge.

In Chapter 5 you will learn about a dog's temperament.

Chapter 5:
A Dog's Temperament

As your puppy grows into a dog, you will come to learn his temperament. If you are buying an older dog, the previous owner (or shelter) may be able to tell you about his temperament.

A dog's temperament is the manner in which your dog thinks, behaves, and reacts. Obviously, you want a dog with a good temperament.

Some of a dog's temperament is inherited, but much of it will depend on how he was raised. You could have a well-respected breed, but if he was not raised properly as a puppy, he may not exude a good temperament.

The amount of compassion and attention you give your dog will help with his temperament. As will the way you condition and train him.

So what does a dog's temperament consist of? Trainers and veterinarians have studied a number of traits for years, and typically these traits are a good mixture of both mental and physical traits.

A dog's temperament actually can be tested. In fact, many animal rescue groups test a dog's temperament before it is made available for adoption. They perform a series of tests and the dog is rated on his responses. This is so future owners will know the character of the dog to be able to find the best match possible.
From these temperament tests, trainers can identify if a dog is responsive, nervous, aggressive, independent, etc.

In this chapter we will look at some of the more common temperament characteristics.

Temperament Characteristics

Aggression

When a dog shows aggression, he is using a means of defense. There are two types of defense—attack and retreat. A dog with an attack aggression assumes all people, excluding his owner, is an enemy.

A dog who retreats will withdraw from the situation. It is ideal for a dog to be in the middle of the range—one that will never attack or retreat, but will be even tempered with everyone.

Animal Aggression

Animal aggression is not a good trait for your dog and it is hard to correct once it has been established. Dogs will fight over food, social status, and sexual rivalry. They also love to chase other animals. These situations surface the instinctive animal aggression of dogs that lived in the wild.

There are two very common reasons for animal aggression. The first is reason is when a dog was not given the opportunity for plenty of socialization as a puppy. The second reason is that he was not corrected and handled properly by his owner when the aggression first started. As a dog owner, you need to watch for signs of animal aggression and then take the steps to prevent it from developing.

Anxiety

This is a fear that a dog exhibits when he becomes extremely concerned about something. You will notice this if your dog begins to pant very rapidly. A dog will demonstrate this anxiety when he has an unpleasant or shocking experience. He can also show anxiety if he lives in a home where there is a lot of tension and arguments. However, when the tension lifts and the arguments go away, the dog will usually return to normal.

Attentiveness

All dogs possess this natural characteristic, but some have more of it than others. Attentiveness needs to be developed and this can be done through regular and disciplined training.

Apprehensive Aggression

Dogs with this trait are usually suspicious or nervous. They also exhibit aggression, sometimes protective aggression. They are oftentimes referred to as "fear biters" but are only likely to bite when they are frightened or cornered.

Body Sensitivity

This is a very important characteristic to be aware of when you are training your dog to walk on a leash. Some dogs have are highly sensitive and a light tug on the leash is all they need to respond.

Other dogs with lower body sensitivity won't respond as well. This lower body sensitivity would result from small, light tugs over a lengthy period of time. The dog has become so "immune" to the tugs that when a firm tug is given, it doesn't affect him in the slightest.

Capacity to Learn

Some breeds have a greater capacity to learn than others. However, if a dog has a good temperament—no matter what breed he belongs to—he will usually have a good capacity to learn. Even dogs in the breeds with a high capacity to learn will learn at different rates—some will learn quickly and some learn slowly.

Concentration

This characteristic develops gradually over time after the dog has participated in training for a few weeks. Before training, he has nothing to really focus on, so it would be unfair to say *"my dog can't concentrate"* if he has not had any training.

A dog with good concentration will focus on the task at hand whether it is training, walking on a leash, or playing. A dog with poor concentration looks around with no specific purpose or focus.

With a good trainer, a dog's concentration can be developed to an extent, but the dog also needs to have a willingness to concentrate.

Curiosity

A curious dog is one that can more easily conquer his fears. If a dog shows signs of curiosity, over time he will become braver as you encourage him to approach things that cause him fear.

Dominance & Submissiveness

The dominance characteristic goes back to dogs living in large packs and their position on the social status ladder. The most dominant dog was always the leader.

If you are going to have more than one dog in your house, it is best if you have two dogs that are not on the same "step" of the ladder. For example, fights are more likely to develop between two leader-type dogs or two very submissive dogs.

Energy

Every dog has his own mental and physical energy level. Some dogs have so much energy that it is almost impossible for the owner to control him. Other dogs have very little energy, so they need a lot of motivation.

Dogs with an abundance of energy can burn off some of this through excessive and disciplined training. This will help the dog be productive and settle down.

Excitability

Puppies are usually very excitable and this is perfectly normal. If a puppy never shows signs of excitement, there could be something seriously wrong.

Older dogs show excitability when they have been indoors for a long period of time or if there is a lot of tension in the home. For dogs that show excessive excitability, make sure that he is taken out often for walks. Be sure to remain calm when you are controlling him. Yelling at him or exerting force on him will only make him more excited.

Hearing Sensitivity

Hearing sensitivity is similar to body sensitivity in that it can fall anywhere between low and high. Most dogs have a hearing sensibility that is in the medium to high range.

Therefore, dogs are quite receptive to your voice tone. If you use too harsh of tone and volume on a highly sensitive dog, then he could be heartbroken. This makes it a real challenge to train.

Dogs with a very low hearing sensitivity are also quite difficult to train. They get like this when their owner has been inconsistent with their training or when the owner is a real nag. They eventually start to ignore their owner.

Jealousy

The jealousy trait was also discussed back in Chapter One. Jealously usually rises when the owner is giving their attention to another dog. Jealously can eventually lead to aggression

Protective Aggression

It is very natural for a dog to become protective of their owners and their home.
They can become protective of other possessions inside and outside of the house too.

Some owners unintentionally allow their dogs to become too protective, or even encourage the behavior. However, too much protection can actually be quite dangerous.

Stubbornness

A stubborn dog is one that will just sit there and not do anything that you want him to. This can make training exercises very difficult. As an owner you need to exercise your authority and when your dog participates in the training, award him.

In this chapter, you learned about how temperament problems can be both inherited and learned traits. Most of the traits listed can be corrected with extensive training.

Chapter 6:
Prepare For Training

As you prepare for training it is important that you understand some basic training principles. Whether you have a new puppy who is training for the first time, or you have an older dog that needs to unlearn some less-than-desirable habits, you will benefit from learning some basic training principles.

In this chapter, you will learn some essentials that will help you prepare for training including basic training principles and helpful equipment.

A Brief Summary of Training Methods

There are different methods of dog training available today. Here is a brief summary of the most popular.

Positive Reinforcement Dog Training

Positive dog training is any method that is used to reward positive behavior in a positive manner. This does not include training used with dangerous choker collars, devices that give the dog an electrical shock, yelling, or hitting—these training methods are inhumane and should not be used on your dog!

Positive dog training is rewarding your dog with lots of love, treats, playtime, car rides, belly rubs, pets, massages, or anything that your dog finds exciting. Your dog will learn quickly from positive dog training once he associates his good behavior with rewards! This E-book is based on positive behavior-based dog training.

Clicker Training

Clicker training is also positive dog training and is a very effective training method. Interestingly, clicker training was originally used for dolphin training. By using a small handheld clicker, you "click" whenever your dog does something you approve of, and then give him a treat immediately.

This training method is so effective because the sound is immediate—faster than your voice. This is a fun method for both you and your dog. For you, you will see positive results quicker. For your dog, he will associate the clicker sound with treats! Clicker training is effective for the young puppy to the older dog. To apply clicker training to the teachings in this E-book, simply click before giving your dog the treat or other reward.

Dog Whispering

This is another positive technique that was originally used for horse training, but is becoming more popular with dog training. This training enables you to use your knowledge of your dog's body language and actions to better communicate with him in a way that makes sense to him. This is used more for higher-level training than the training in this E-book.

Lead and Collar Training

These are collars that correct a dog's actions by tightening briefly and adding pressure when you tug on the lead. If you choose this type of training, the collar should only be used for training and never leave the dog unattended when he is wearing it as it could cause injury or even strangulation if it gets caught on something. This type of training should only be used by someone who knows what they are doing and is sincere about the dog's well being.

Whistle Training

Whistle training is a specialized form of training that is best implemented with the assistance of a professional trainer. It is mainly used for distance control when hunting or shooting. In these situations, a dog is better able to hear the sound of a whistle, than the owner's voice.

Basic Training Principles

As you learned in the Introduction, you will need to build a trusting relationship with your dog for your training to be effective. Your dog craves your love and attention more than anything and this desire is very useful in training.

All training should be conducted with lots of patience and loads of energy. Your dog should find training fun—he wants to please you! You should never yell or hit your dog.

Always use your dog's name before giving a command or when praising, never when you are correcting. For example, "Rover, sit. Yes, good boy. Good Rover!"

Below are some other basic training principles you should follow as you begin to train your dog.

Praise and Correction

Your dog will not know whether he is doing something right or wrong unless you tell him. Teach him early that training is about praise and correction.

You should always praise your dog when he does something right—and do it immediately. If you wait longer than three seconds to praise him, he will most likely forget what he is being rewarded for!

A reward is anything that your dog gets excited about, such as treats, petting, praising words, playtime, food, a walk, a car ride, etc.

The training in this E-book is behavior-based. Positive behavior is praised and wrong behavior is corrected or ignored. Each time a behavior is rewarded, he will most likely repeat that same behavior.

Discouraging Negative Behavior

Even if you practice hours upon hours of training with your dog, he will still behave inappropriately on occasion. Therefore, you need to make him aware when he is behaving badly.

Following are some ways to discourage negative behavior:

- **Correction –** This is when you stop a bad behavior and replace it with a correct behavior.

Let's say you are walking your dog on a leash and you approach another dog. Your dog tries to jump, so you correct him immediately by saying "no" while simultaneously tugging lightly on the leash. Then you say "heel." After he heels, praise him. This exercise let's the dog know what he did wrong and what he should do instead.

- **Verbal reprimand –** Choose a word that you can say that will indicate to your dog that he should stop whatever it is he is doing. It could be "no," "hey," "eh-eh," "enough," etc.

When you use a verbal reprimand, don't yell it or say it in an angry tone. Instead, just say it in a short and sharp tone that will capture his attention.
When you see your dog doing something he shouldn't such as chewing on a plant, say your verbal reprimand word and redirect his behavior to another activity. Once your dog gets used to this command, he will automatically redirect himself to another activity.

- **Ignore him** – If your dog is an excessive barker, ignore him! Obviously, you can't ignore the sound, but you can turn your head away from him, show no reaction, or leave the room.

If you do this consistently, your dog will come to realize that by barking, he doesn't gain your attention, but instead he loses it. And since your dog craves your attention, he will want to do whatever he can to get it—even if that means no barking!

- **Time out** – This is a quick 30 second time out in a crate, small room or space, or a tie-down of a short leash attached to a permanent object. If your dog misbehaves and no other types of reprimands work, you can give him a time out. If it is longer than 30 seconds, the punishment will actually be ineffective.

If he is barking during time out, wait until he stops before you let him out. Otherwise, he will bark even longer and louder the next time you give him a time out! It may take several time outs before your dog understands what it means, but once he does, this is a great way to discourage negative behavior.

Using Your Voice

The way you use your voice tone has a significant amount of impact on your training. Your dog may not necessarily understand the words that you are saying, but he can definitely understand the way in which you are saying them.

Commands should be said in a very meaningful tone—as if what you are saying at that particular moment is the most important thing. You want to say it with a positive tone so he is interested, but don't say it too enthusiastically or he might think he is being praised.

When he performs the command correctly, then you can praise him lavishly with "good boy" "Good Rover" in a very loving way. When you need to correct your dog with a "no," it should be firm and short, but not loudly or angrily.

Consistency is Key

In order for your dog to learn your rules of training, you will need to show consistency.

You will need to enforce your rules consistently, as well as everyone else in the family. This means that everyone must correct misbehavior and praise positive behavior—and everyone must have the same rules. For example, if mom and dad correct the dog when he jumps on the sofa, then the kids should also. It will be very confusing if some of the family lets him sit on the sofa and some do not.

All the rules must be very easy for the dog to understand and learn. You want to set your dog up for achievement, not failure.

Timing is Everything

As important as consistency is in training, so is the timing. Dogs live very much in the present moment. You must always praise and correct the dog at the time of the action.

For example, if you stumble across an accident that your dog made in the house, it will do him no good if you say "No" to him after the fact. However, if you catch your dog in the act of making an accident, then you can say "No" and direct him to the outside.

The same is true for a positive behavior. If you ask your dog to "sit" and he does successfully, if you walk to the other side of the house to grab a treat, by the time you get back, he will have forgotten what it was you are rewarding him for. Rather, he will actually associate the treat with whatever he is doing right at that moment.

Constant Supervision

Because you want to set your dog up for success, you need to keep a close eye on him at all times. Keep him around you so you can look for opportunities to reward him and correct him when he is doing something wrong.

Most likely your dog will follow you around the house, but if he doesn't you should consider using puppy gates to keep him in a certain area or close the door to the room you are in.

When you make time to supervise and reward your dog for doing a job well done, he will want to be by your side. Again, your dog wants to please you and he wants your love and attention.

Training an Older Dog versus a Puppy

They say "you can't teach an old dog new tricks." But this isn't necessarily true. Indeed, an older dog can be more difficult to train, but that shouldn't deter you from bringing one into your home.

If you have adopted a dog from a shelter, you probably don't know much about his background. Maybe he was a runaway. Maybe he was too much for the previous dog to handle. Maybe he is disobedient or maybe he is very trainable.

A young puppy is relatively easy to train if you start training him before he has a chance to develop any bad habits. Training is fun for the pup and he loves being rewarded!

An older dog misbehaves because he hasn't received proper training. However, he most likely already understands the meaning of "no" and other basic commands. The best thing you can do is to begin training as soon as you bring him into your home. You need to establish that you (or another adult) is the alpha leader, otherwise he will assume the role.

The main difference between training an older dog compared to a puppy is that an older dog may be slower to respond—mentally and physically. Just like humans, the young are full of energy and the older are a little slower, and perhaps have a few aches and pains!

While a puppy could train for great lengths at a time (as long as the rewards keep coming!) you need to give an older dog more breaks, again—mentally and physically.

You will need to understand the characteristics of the dog's breed and pay close attention to the older dog's temperament and body language—even more so than with an ambitious young puppy. Paying attention to these things will give you clues on what he is thinking.

Training Equipment

A major component in successful training is the equipment that you use. There are many types of collars, leashes, muzzles, and crates. Use the information below to help you gain an understanding of their uses, then determine the type that you think will be most beneficial and comfortable for your dog.

Collars

There are a variety of different collars available. Choose the one that is most appropriate for your dog and his needs.

Flat or Buckle Collar

This type of collar is fit around the dog's neck. These are available in a variety of materials such as nylon, leather, and cloth. This collar is good for basic restraint for dogs that do not pull forcefully on a leash when walking. If he pulls too hard on the leash, he will choke or gag against the force of the collar. If you need to train your dog not to pull on a leach, this is probably not your best collar.

Halter or Head Collar

This type of collar is fitted on the dog's muzzle and neck. It basically serves the same purpose as a halter on a horse, meaning when his head goes in one direction, his body will follow in the same direction.

The head collar does not use very much force so there is very little pain for the dog, yet there is a maximum amount of control so the dog will move in the direction you want him to.

A head collar can be somewhat uncomfortable for a dog to wear. Some dogs don't accept a head collar, even when he has been wearing it for several weeks. For example, they may stand still and refuse movement, or they may try to remove it with their paws or other objects. A dog owner prefers a head collar because it significantly reduces pulling by the dog— when the dog has been trained not to pull.

Martingale

This is a slip collar that looks like a typical collar yet it can only be tightened to a certain point. This way, the dog will be comfortable, but it will also give the owner a fair amount of control. This is a very easy collar to fit. It can either be slid over the dog's head, or it can snap around the dog's neck.

An advantage to a Martingale collar is that it can not be easily removed from the dog's neck—even if he is pulling backwards. It has a restricted range of tightness that prevents the dog from choking. However, the Martingale does not work effectively if the dog is a consistent puller.
The Martingale is useful for dogs that tend to pull a little on the leash, but they are discouraged from it. It takes good timing on the trainer's part for the color to work most effectively.

Choke Collar

A choke collar is a training collar that should only be used for extreme cases of aggressive training. This collar tightens around the dog's neck when it is jerked. The tension is released when you let up. A choke collar can be very dangerous if it is not used properly. If you choose to use this type of collar in training, it is essential that you know how to use it and that you use it with the utmost care. If you don't, you could traumatize and hurt your dog.

Harnesses

A harness is a device that wraps to the dog's body, with the leash attached at the top of the dog's back at the shoulder blades. This is different than a collar because a collar only controls a dog at the neck or head. A harness distributes the dog's pulling force evenly across his chest and shoulders, which can actually allow the dog to pull even harder.

There are also no -pull harnesses which puts pressure on the dog between his armpits, or the area between his front legs and chest when the leash tightens. This can cause abrasions on the armpits if it is not fitted properly.

There are several styles of harnesses to choose from, so pick the one that is most comfortable to the dog. The regular harnesses are usually pain-free for the dog and are useful for dogs that have had previous neck injuries.

The disadvantage of harnesses is that when they are used to stop pulling by medium to large dog, they are not very effective. They are able to use their legs and chest to create force to pull against the leash. However, they can work well for small dogs because since the dogs are so low to the ground, they really can't pull against it.

Leashes

A leash is simply a length of material that attaches to the dog's collar or harness. It is used to restrain the dog and keep him safe. There are a wide variety of leashes to choose from.

- **2-foot leash:** This is a good leash to use when training a dog to walk close to its owner.

- **6-foot leash:** This is also a good leash for training purposes. It gives just enough space for the dog to perform stationary training exercises.

- **Long line leash:** These range from 10-40 feet are usually made from a cotton wedding or nylon material. The longer line is beneficial for training control from farther distances.

- **Retractable leash:** This leash lets you adjust the length of leash, depending on what your situation.

Leashes are available in several different materials, including:

- **Chain:** This is almost impossible for a dog to destroy and it is fairly inexpensive. However, it is heavy and it can be uncomfortable for the owner if the leash hits him or wraps around his leg.

- **Cotton webbing/rope:** This is light in weight, very easy to handle, and very inexpensive. However, it is easy for dogs to chew through and it can callous the owner's hand.

- **Leather:** This is a fairly sturdy leash that is easy to hold, especially as it softens over time with use. However, dogs can easily chew through it and it can be more expensive.

- **Nylon:** This is very durable and it is quite difficult for a dog to chew through. They come in a variety of weights and thickness.

These are the leashes that come in many colors and patterns and they are relatively inexpensive.

Muzzles

A muzzle is a leather or wire restraining device that fits over the dog's snout to prevent him from biting. A muzzle is useful if your dog is in pain to keep him from lashing out and biting.

Muzzles come in a variety of sizes, so if you have the need for one, make sure it fits your dog appropriately.

Crates

You will find that crates are a major component in your training efforts, particularly house training.

There are many types of crates on the market to choose from. Most are either wire or plastic. Wire crates are durable and allow for plenty of ventilation.

Plastic crates are lighter in weight so they can be moved easily from room to room or traveling. Refer to the "Selecting a Crate" section back in Chapter 3 for more information about types and sizes of crates.

In this chapter you learned some of basic principles of training that will help have the right mindset as you read about training in the next few chapters.

In Chapter 10, you will learn about basic obedience training.

Chapter 7:
Basic Obedience Training

So far in this E-book you have learned a lot about dogs including their psychology, different breeds, their temperament, their body language, and more. Now that you understand the basics of how they think and act, you can begin training.

This chapter will cover some of the most basic training commands. Set aside plenty of time a day to practice these commands.

Start with one or two a day, and as he masters those commands gradually add more commands. You will need to continually practice the previous training exercises he has learned, so there may be days that you practice all training commands.

Ideally, you will practice the commands at any given time, even when you are not in an actual "training session." Incorporate training into your everyday life.

For example, when you are getting ready for work, when you are cooking dinner, and when you are watching television. Any opportunity you have to train your dog—train him!

The "Sit" Command

Stand facing your dog with a yummy treat held between your right thumb and index finger, with your palm facing up. Hold the treat in front of your dog at his nose.

Raise your right hand with the treat slightly above your dog's head then move your hand back over his head. Your dog will have his eyes locked on the treat, so he will most likely sit to keep his balance. Immediately as he sits, reward him with the treat and praise him with a "Yes, good boy," or "Yes, good Rover."

At this point you are not yet saying the command. Repeat this exercise several times. Once you are confident that he will sit every time you do the hand motion, start saying the command with "Rover sit."

Repeat this exercise several times at different locations throughout the house and back yard. The more distractions there are the better because this will help your dog with his concentration level. Once your dog is comfortable with the "sit" command without a leash, you can add his leash. Knowing the "sit" command on a leash will be important when you are outside on walks.

The "Down" Command

Now that your dog knows the "sit" command, the down command will be a snap! Start by luring your dog into the "sit" position. Hold a treat in your right hand between your thumb and index finger, with your palm facing down towards the floor. Your hand will be in front of your dog's nose.

Lower your hand slowly to the floor behind your dog's right paw and then back towards his buttocks. When you lower the food on at an angle to the floor, keep it close to your dog's body. Your dog will follow the lure and he will lie down on his hip. (This is called a "relaxed down" which is a safe and stable position for the dog's body.)

Once he is lowered all the way to the floor, give him the treat. Repeat this several times until you are confident that he will go down every time.

Once he does, start adding his name and the command, such as "Rover down." Once he is lying down, reward him with the treat and give him words of praise such as "Yes, Rover, good boy!"

Repeat this exercise several times at different locations throughout the house and in the backyard. Make sure there are plenty of distractions around so you can work on his concentration too.

Once he has mastered the "down" command, put him on the leash and practice it while walking.

The "Off" Command

The "off" command differs from the "down" command in that you use "off" when you want your dog to get off of a person or piece of furniture.

This command is especially useful for when you or visitors walk through the front door. Your dog may get so excited that he stands on his two hind legs, with his two front legs up on you or the visitor.

To practice this command, have a treat in your right hand and hold it up high and close to your body. Your dog will try to reach up for it, so move your right arm with the treat to the right and down. When your dog has all four legs on the ground, verbally praise him and give him the treat. Once you are confident that he will get down every time, start saying "Rover, off" right before he is down. Then praise him and give him a treat.

Repeat this exercise several times at different locations throughout the house, especially at all of the doors, where this behavior will most likely happen.

Walking on a Leash

Walking nicely on a leash is something that will take some practice with your dog. Dog pulling is a common problem and unless it is corrected at an early age, it will get harder to correct the older the dog gets.

When you allow your dog to pull without any correction, your dog will believe that it is ok to pull. And since you continue your walk, he will think he's being rewarded for pulling! This is obviously not the message you want to send him.

If your dog pulls and you pull him back, he will only continue to pull harder. This will be fun for him! Therefore, you need to train him to walk properly on the leash.

Before you start walking, stand still and hold the leash with both hands and several treats. Keep your hands close to your body. Whenever your dog looks up at you, praise him and give him a treat. Or, if he is just sitting or standing still, praise him and give him a treat. You want him to know that this is good. He will soon notice that the act of paying attention to you is rewarded.

If your dog begins to lean forward or start to walk forward, lean your body backwards or take a few steps backwards, but don't pull back. Hold your hands against your body and stand still. There may be tension on the leash, but just wait. Once your dog slackens his pull, or when he looks up to you, give him verbal praise and extend your arm down by your side and give him a treat.

Continue to praise your dog until he moves forward toward the end of the leash. If he pulls to the point where there is tension, don't say anything. Once your dog releases the tension, then you can once again praise him.

When your dog resumes standing position next to you, you can begin to walk. Say your dog's name and the command "let's go" or "let's walk" and begin to walk forward. This command should be spoken right before the dog moves forward.

If your dog walks properly without pulling forward, continue to walk and reward him periodically with verbal praise and tasty treats. If you see that your dog is about to pull forward, stop walking and stand still. Your dog will wonder why you stopped walking so he will look back at you. Once he does this verbally praise him, give him a great, and give him a treat as you start to walk forward. Repeat this whenever your dog is about to pull forward.

It will not take him long to realize that when his collar is tight, you won't follow him, rather the walking stops. Therefore, he will want to walk lightly.

In the early stages of this training exercise you will want to practice this in your home or backyard. This way, your dog will have a chance to get used to walking on the leash in a controlled environment. Then, once he is comfortable here, you can walk him on the sidewalk.

As mentioned in the last chapter, you want to set your dog up for success, not failure. So you want to give him every opportunity to be rewarded. Because this training exercise will take a lot of practice at first, you may want to use pieces of kibble rather than treats. You can take him on a walk during one of his meal times and give him his meal this way. Once your dog can walk without needing a lot of correction and reward, you can start giving him treats instead.

The "Stay" Command

The "stay" command is an important one for your dog to know. Additionally, it is one that will test your dog's patience because the dog will need to remain in the "stay" position until you release him.

Begin by giving your dog the "sit" command. Then say "stay" while giving him a hand signal of your hand flat in front of him with your palm facing him. Give him verbal praise and stand still for a couple of seconds, then give him a treat, wait a couple seconds, and then release him with an "ok" to allow him to get up out of position. Repeat this exercise and each time add on another second, up to 5 seconds in the sit position.

Once your dog is comfortable with the 5 second "stay," then you will be able to build up to a 10 second "stay." To do this, ask your dog to "sit." Right when he sits, give the command to "stay." Verbally praise him calmly and give him a treat and continue to praise him as you give him another treat. It is fine to give him two or three treats during a 10 second "stay."

Your dog will quickly learn that staying still equals a treat! However, if your dog starts to move from the sit position, tell him in an unemotional tone "eh-eh," "wrong," or "no." Remove the treat from his view and ask him to "sit" again.

If he still does not sit, take the treat and lure him again into the sit position, but don't give him the treat. Once he is sitting again, say "stay" again and repeat the exercise. If your dog continues to get up during this training exercise, you may be moving too quickly for him. Again, you want your dog to succeed, so it is better to go back to shorter intervals and work on those again, than to push him to do something he is not ready for yet.

If your dog has been succeeding consistently at the 10 second "stay," you can now try something new. As your dog is in the sit position, begin to walk around your dog slowly, staying close to him. He will be watching you and will probably want to get up, so say "stay" every 90 degrees of the circle you are making. Praise him for staying still and give him a treat.

Again, if your dog tries to move from position, say "eh-eh," "wrong," or "no." Then, if he stays seated, praise him, and remind him to "stay." Don't give a treat when you release him from the command. The reward is for the action of "staying" not "moving."

Practice this exercise around the house and in the backyard—in a controlled environment at first, then with lots of distractions. Next, try it when you are out for a walk. However, this should only be done if you are very confident in his ability to succeed.

The "Come" Command

The "come" is perhaps one of the most important commands that you want your dog to know—and one of the most difficult for him to learn. When you need to use the "come" command it might be when he has ran out of the house or when he is in a dangerous situation.

Therefore, in order for the "come" command to be effective, you need to stay calm, no matter how frightened you may be for his safety. If you run after him in a panic, he will only run faster and farther away. If you stay calm, your dog will more likely move towards you.

The "come" command should only be given for a very positive experience and you should praise him lavishly when he responds correctly.

For example, if you say "Rover, come" and then you give him a bath, he will associate "come" with a bad experience (if he doesn't like baths.) Or, if you say "Rover, come" and point out an accident that he made three hours ago and you scold him, he will associate the "come" command with a scolding.

Therefore, every time you use the "come" command there should be a positive reward and lots of praising words waiting for him. He should want to come to you no matter where he is or what he is doing. The best way for your dog to learn the "come" command is through practice, practice, and more practice. Start by standing on the other side of a room from your dog. Say "Rover, come." As soon as he comes all the way up to you praise him "yes Rover, good boy!" and give him a treat.

Repeat this as often as you can. He will quickly realize that you have a hand full of treats and will sit right by you so try different things. For example, go to another room and say "Rover, come." If he comes, praise him and reward him.

You could also try practicing this exercise down a long hallway or from another side of the house. Have another family member help you and you can make a fun game out of it, sort of like "hide and seek."

There are many ways that you can practice this command, but the key is to practice it often and always have a positive reward waiting for your dog. It doesn't have to be a treat; it could also be a toy, a walk, a belly rub, etc.

If you are in a situation, for example you are out in your front yard, your dog is loose and he does not respond to your "come" command, he might not fully understand it yet. In that case, you could try a couple of other options.
First, you could offer him a treat "Rover, do you want a treat?" Be sure to say it enthusiastically and will hopefully come running to you in excitement.

Second, you could try to ignore your dog. For example, he may want you to chase him. But if you ignore him instead, he will wonder what it is you have found that is more interesting than him, so he may come up to you.

A loose dog can be a frightening situation, so the more you can practice this exercise, the more your dog will trust that you have a wonderful reward waiting for him!

The "Wait" Command

You learned the release word "ok" to use when your dog has finished a command, now you will learn "wait" which puts your dog "on hold" and to stop what he is doing.

This command is particularly important to use at doors—whether it is your house door, your car door, the door at the veterinary's office, etc. It is also useful for the driveway or curb. For example, you might say "Rover wait" before walking through a door, then when you open the door you say "ok!" so he knows he can walk through it.

To practice this training exercise, you will want to attach your dog's leash to his collar. Approach the door slowly and then stop before opening it. Give the "sit" command. Once he sits, praise him and reward him.

Then, open the door slightly. If he tries to move towards the door, close it calmly and try it again. Continue practicing this exercise until he stays in position and does not move toward the door as you open it.

Once you are confident that you can open the door without him moving towards it, try it again and now open the door wide. Give the "sit" command and walk in front of your dog so you are now facing him. Praise him as you do this. You are blocking him from walking through the door, so he should not be able to step forward. If he tries to get around you, shut the door, or step forward to block his path, and then try again.

Now, step to the end of your leash. Continue to praise him until you get to the end of the leash. If your dog moves forward, again block his path. When you get to the end of your leash, you can release him with "ok!"
Once you are confident that your dog can execute the command consistently, start using "Rover, wait" with your hand signal.

Practice this training exercise at each door and then try it outside on a sidewalk, but only after he has convinced you that you can trust him.

In the next chapter you will learn how to use the more advanced "wait" command at the food bowl.

In this chapter, you learned some of the basic dog training commands that you can teach your puppy or dog. Once he

gains confidence, he will be ready for some more advanced commands.

In Chapter 8 you will learn some more advanced training commands.

Chapter 8:
Advanced Obedience Training

Now that your dog is a pro at basic obedience training, he can begin advanced obedience training!

It is important to not try and teach your dog too much too fast. If you need to spend one, two, three, or more months on the basic training, then by all means, do so. It will be much better for your dog's self-confidence if you train slowly and consistently, than quickly and randomly. But, there will be a point when your dog is ready for the challenge, so let's begin!

The "Wait" Command at the Food Bowl

In the previous chapter, your dog learned how to wait at a doorway or curbside. Now, you will teach him how to wait at his food bowl. With the temptation of his favorite kibble right in front of him, he will need to learn patience!

Give the "sit" command and then say "wait" while simultaneously placing a treat on the floor in front of him. If your dog goes for the treat, remove it quickly and say "wait."

After a couple seconds of waiting, praise him and release him with "ok" and let him have the treat.

Practice this exercise several times and then increase by one second. Repeat several times and then increase by another second. Continue this until he can patiently wait for 5 seconds before getting a treat.

Now, once he has succeeded with treats, let's apply the same exercise with his food bowl. Hold the food bowl and say "wait."

Lower the bowl to the floor and if your dog moves towards it, remove the bowl quickly and say "wait." After a couple of seconds waiting, praise him and release him with "ok."

Practice this training exercise for every meal that you give him. If he starts to jump at the dish while the bowl is in your hands, try the treat exercise again.

The "Leave It" Command

The "leave it" command is different from the "wait" command. "Leave it" means you don't want your dog to go near something. "Wait" as you recall, means a temporary pause.

You will want to use the "leave it" command if there is something on the floor that you don't want your dog to go near, such as food, a pill, broken glass, etc.
To practice "leave it," put a little distance between you and your dog and place a treat on the floor in front of you. If your dog starts to move toward the treat, cover it immediately with your hand or foot. Once your dog stops, say "yes" and give him another treat from your hand.

Your dog should get the idea that if he looks at you, rather than go for the treat, he will still get a treat! Once he has the hang of that, start saying the command "leave it" right when you toss the treat on the floor.

Your dog will learn that "leave it" means come to you—not go for the treat. If your dog avoids the treat on the floor by looking at you, looking away from the treat, or turning his head in the opposite direction, give him verbal praise and a reward. Let him have the treat by saying "take it."

With a lot of practice, your dog will be able to resist touching anything!

Walking on the Leash: The Right-About Turn

By now your dog is comfortable walking on a leash. Now, we're going to advance his walking capabilities.

The right-about turn is a 180 degree turn that you would do walking in a straight line, then turning around to walk back. It is a good idea to do this right-turn about often when walking, so he knows that you are leading the way.

As you approach your turning point, switch the leash from your right hand to your left hand. This way, you can pat your right leg with your right hand. Make a sharp turn as you pat your leg. You may need to give the leash a slight tug as you turn.

Keep the leash loose at all times. If you pull on it, your dog will pull away. Practice this several times. Once he has the hang of it, start adding the command "turn," "heel" or "pivot" as you pat your leg and make the sharp turn. Praise him immediately. Then you can return the leash to your right hand.

Practice the right-about turn often when you are walking your dog and keep him on his toes!

Walking on the Leash: The Right Turn

The right turn will be very easy for your dog once he knows the right-about turn. The only difference between the two commands is that this is a 90 degree turn, whereas the right-about was a 180 degree turn.

As with the right-about turn, sharp turns work better than slow and wide turns. When he turns correctly, praise him.

Walking on the Leash: The Left Turn

The left turn is usually easier for dog owners because they can keep the leash in the right hand at all times. When you are ready to turn, grab the leash with your left hand, slightly tug the leash backing line with the dog's spine, while pivoting on the ball of your left foot towards the left, and bring your right foot around and continue walking. Then, let go of the leash with your left hand.

It is important to keep on walking and not stopping when you step around with your right foot. As your dog sees you turn your body, his body will follow. If you accidentally step with your left dog first, you might step on his paws.

When your dog correctly turns consistently for several times, start adding the command "turn," "heel" or "pivot" as you are about to turn. Always praise him when he turns correctly.

Fun Tricks

Every dog needs to know some fun tricks! Here are a few that will keep him and his audience—entertained!

Circle

Start with your dog facing you. Take a treat and lead his nose to the right and around your body, slowly. He will follow the treat behind your back and to the front. Once he has completed the full circle, praise him and give him a treat. After he does several successful circles, add the word "circle" right when you begin to move the treat around your body.

Crawl

Begin by giving your dog the "down" command so he lying all the way down on the floor. Hold a treat in front of his nose and pull it back towards you. You will probably need to take a few steps back. As he is inching towards you, praise him and give him a treat. After he has done this several times without standing up, add the word "crawl" as you begin to move the treat away from his nose.

Fetch

Begin by holding your dog on the ground and show him the ball. Toss the ball a few feet in front of you. If he doesn't run to get the ball himself, toss it again but this time run with him. Once he starts to return it to you every time, start adding the word "fetch." Of course, praise him and reward him every time he brings you the ball.

Once your dog gets skilled at "fetch," you can teach him to fetch certain objects such as a newspaper, slippers, etc.

Kiss

This is an easy trick, especially if your dog loves to lick your face! Whenever he licks your face, say "give me a kiss." Praise him and reward him.

Play Dead

Start by giving the "down" command. Once he is on his tummy, gently roll his body so he is lying on his side. Hold his head and body in place for a few seconds. Then, say "ok" and let him stand up to get his reward. After he does this successfully several times, start adding the words "play dead" as you roll him on his side.

Roll Over

Begin by giving the "down" command. Once your dog is on his tummy, kneel down beside him, holding a treat above his nose. Once he is staring at the treat, move it around and behind his head. He will follow you by lying on his side and then he will roll over completely. Praise him and reward him with the treat. Once he has this trick mastered, start adding the words "roll over" as you move the treat behind his head.

Shake

First, give your dog the "sit" command. Then, grab his paw with your hand and hold it for a few seconds. Then praise him and give him a treat. Once he starts to do this regularly, add the word "shake." Eventually he will be able to do it without you grabbing his paw.

Once your dog is confident, he will be ready for advanced obedience training—and he can even learn some fun new tricks along the way! As you have noticed throughout all the training exercise, repetition, consistency, praise, and reward are essential.

In the next chapter you will learn about crate training.

Chapter 9:
Crate Training

Crate training is a valuable training tool that is beneficial for training young puppies and adult dogs alike. No matter what age your dog is, you will come to find that a crate can be used for many purposes.

A crate acts like a private "den" for your dog—a safe and secure place that he can go to anytime of the day. For you, the dog owner, the crate is a safe and secure place for you to keep him when you are away from home.

A crate is a safe place to keep your dog when you need to leave the house. If you do not place him in a crate, your dog will not know what to do or how to act.
Therefore, he will become anxious and nervous and will take this nervous energy out on your rugs, plants, furniture, etc. He will do all of those bad habits that a dog does when he is scared or bored: dig, bark, chew, destroy, attempt to escape, pace back and forth, etc.

Your dog's response to the crate will all depend on how you introduce him to it. (Refer back to Chapter 3.) You want his crate to be his most favorite place in the whole wide world, so make it a positive experience every time he goes near it.

In this chapter you will learn how to maximize the value of the crate by learning how to use it in training your dog.

Benefits to Crate Training

You've already learned that crate training is a safe place for your dog.
Other benefits include:

- A crate can help prevent behaviors such as digging and chewing, because it will serve as a "time out" spot.

- A crate provides as a safe sleeping environment for your dog so he stays put in one place at night.

- A crate can be used when you can't watch a puppy for a certain amount of time.

- A crate is helpful in your dog's house training, which you will learn about in the next chapter.

- A crate helps your dog adjust to a regular schedule for sleeping, going outside, etc.

- A crate is transportable so it can be moved from room to room, so your dog can always be with the rest of the family no matter where they are.

- A crate can be easily transported in a car or airplane.

In order for a crate to be beneficial in any of these ways, you need to help your dog adjust to it.

Adjusting to a Crate

As you learned in Chapter 3, the dog's first experience with a crate should be positive. Once you bring him home, you will introduce him to his crate.
Have some treats and toys waiting inside, with the door closed. Walk him to his crate and he will see the goodies inside. Once he is

pawing at the crate, open it up and say "yes, good boy" and let him walk inside. Don't close the crate door yet, just praise him for walking inside.

When he exits the crate, don't praise him. You don't want him to think that being outside of the crate is better than being inside the crate. Never force your dog inside the crate. He will interpret that as a form of punishment. So if you need to, toss in more treats.

Repeat the exercise a few times, each time increasing the amount of time that your dog is inside the crate. Continue to praise him. Then, start shutting the door behind him.

He may whine or bark and try to get out. If he does this, wait until he stops, then open the door to let him out. If you let him out while he is still whining or barking, he will think that you are rewarding his bad behavior. Let him in again, but this time for a shorter amount of time.

Once your dog is comfortable walking in and out of the crate, start adding the word "crate." Then, practice the command from farther distances and keep him in for longer periods of time.

For the first few days of crate training, you should increase time by short increments, but never over 30 minutes. The only time that he should be in the crate longer is when it is time for him to go to sleep.

Sleeping in the Crate

The first few nights you have your dog home, you should consider keeping the crate in your bedroom. If this is not possible, keep it in another room that is close to an outside door.

If you are training a new puppy, he will most likely cry during the night to be let outside. If he does cry, take him out.

If your dog cries in the crate and you are positive that he doesn't need to go to the bathroom, but just wants out if his crate, don't let him out while he is barking. If you do this, you will be rewarding him for barking and he will do it every time—longer and louder!

Leaving the House

Once you know your dog is comfortable in a crate during the night, you can begin leaving him in the crate for longer than 30 minutes during the day. Try leaving the house for awhile and see how he reacts.

If you can, listen at the door for any crying or barking. Or, leave a tape recorder so you can tape his vocals.

When you get back, immediately let him out of his crate, again with no praise. Then, let him outside to eliminate.

When you return, look for signs of separation anxiety. Did he have any accidents in his crate? Did he move the crate? Is his chest fur wet from drooling on the floor? Does he greet you frantically like he just had the most horrible experience?

If you see signs of separation anxiety often, you will need to see a professional trainer. Once you and your dog are on a regular routine, the crate will be even more useful.

Using a Crate for Housetraining

A puppy will not want to eliminate where he sleeps, so a crate is an effective tool for controlling your dog's elimination overnight or when you will be away from the house for a few hours.

Always allow your dog to eliminate before placing him in the crate and always allow him to eliminate once he is out of the crate.

If you think it is time for your puppy to eliminate, for example, he just woke up or he just ate and he does not eliminate outside, put him in his crate for 5-10 minutes. When the time passes, take him outside again and use your "go outside" commands. Housetraining with a crate will be explained in more detail in the next chapter.

Tips for using the Crate

The crate can be used as a great time-out tool. If your dog has been misbehaving, place him in the crate for 30 seconds. However, never use the crate to punish your dog for long periods at a time.

Try not to use the crate too often. It is certainly convenient, but if you use it too much, your dog will not get enough socialization with the family or exercise.

If your dog is sick with diarrhea or has been vomiting, don't put him in the crate. Also, if he has bladder or sphincter control problems, you should avoid using the crate until you talk to your veterinarian about the problems (which should be done immediately upon discovering them!)

Before you put your dog in the crate to go to sleep, make sure he has had a chance to eliminate outside. Otherwise, he will cry during the night and he could possibly even have an accident.

Keep the crate in a temperature-controlled environment. It should be neither be too cold or too hot.

Crate training provides as a versatile training tool for so many purposes. If you introduce your dog to it properly, he will love spending time in his own private "den."

In the next chapter, you will learn about housetraining your dog.

Chapter 10: Housetraining

One of the very first training exercises you will want to work on with a new puppy or an adult dog moving into your home is— housetraining! Housetraining is indeed a real test of your patience, but it is one of the first opportunities that you and your puppy will have to bond.

Housetraining is a lot of hard work, but it is necessary. You will need to have a lot of patience and maybe even a sense of humor— as you train your dog. But don't worry, after all of your hard work, you will have a dog that is housetrained!

When it comes to housetraining, every dog succeeds at a different rate. It takes some dogs only a few weeks to learn, where it may take other dogs several months.

Here is perhaps the most important thing to know about housetraining: The rate at which the puppy succeeds is determined by the amount of consistent training that you as the owner give him.

You should begin housetraining your puppy as soon as he arrives home, which is generally around 7 or 8 weeks. It is important to understand that he does not have full sphincter muscle control, so puppies are not able to hold their bladder and bowel movements for very long periods of time.

If your dog is not fully housetrained after one year, you should talk to your veterinarian to make sure there is nothing physically wrong. If there is nothing wrong, then you may want to seek professional training for the housetraining problem.

Although every dog trains at a different success rate, there are many commonalities for general housetraining. This chapter will explain those.

When you prepare for housetraining, keep in mind that consistency and reward are things that you should always do: be consistent with your training efforts and reward success every time!

Training the Older Dog

If you are bringing an older dog into your home that has not yet been housetrained, it may be more of a challenge. Older dogs already have developed their habits, so it will take time to retrain him. However, it can be done!

All of the lessons below can be applied to both the younger and older dog. It may just take longer with the older dog, so be patient. Additionally, older dogs eliminate fewer times than puppies throughout the day, so you have fewer opportunities in the day to train him.

Things to Know about Housetraining

Before you begin housetraining with your dog, there are some basics that you should know. Including:

Where Dogs Won't Eliminate

Dogs develop natural preferences for where they want to eliminate. For example, dogs usually don't want to eliminate where they eat, sleep, and spend their time.

You may be wondering "So why does my dog eliminate on the rug?" The reason is probably because he was expected to "hold it" too long and wasn't let outside. Or, he may have gotten overly excited about something.

Physical Capacity to "Hold It"

Young puppies will need to eliminate every one to two hours during the day when they are active. If your pup has been eating, drinking, playing, or exercising a lot, he may need to go even more. They may or may not be able to hold it throughout the night. Generally, the younger the puppy is, the less he can hold it.

Older dogs that are healthy have the ability to hold it for six to eight hours during the day and eight to ten hours over night.

However, every dog is different so you should track your dog's elimination cycle so you can better estimate when he will need to go out. For example, track his schedule for a couple of weeks.

Then, once you see a pattern, let him out 10-15 minutes before that scheduled time. Of course, he may need to go out more if he has been eating, drinking, playing, or exercising more frequently.

If the situation arises when you need to leave your dog for a longer period than which he can hold it, don't keep him in his crate. Rather, put him in a small room such as a laundry room or bathroom where he can eliminate in an area on newspaper if he needs to, and still keep his sleeping and food area separate.

General Principles of Housetraining

No matter which method you decide to housetrain your dog, you can apply these general principles to help your puppy succeed.

Consistency

It is important for you to be consistent with your dog's routine. This will be one of main rules that help you with housetraining. When your dog has a specific time for eating, sleeping, and playtime, he will more likely succeed in housetraining.

Eating Schedule

A regular eating schedule will give your puppy a predictable appetite, which will help to regulate his digestive processes. What food goes "in" on schedule, it will likely come "out" on schedule.

Obviously, the more food and water you give your puppy, the more he will need to eliminate. Be sure to follow the instructions regarding how much to feed your puppy at which ages and weight level. During the housetraining process, refrain from giving your puppy table scraps, especially if he eats at a different time than the rest of the family because that will throw off his consistent schedule. Also only leave your doggie's food down at meal times for about 20 minutes. Leaving food down throughout the day makes potty training much more difficult to master as it upsets your dog's toileting regime.

After your puppy eats, there will be a very short amount of time before he needs to eliminate. To be safe, take him outside 15 to 20 minutes after he eats. Be sure to give your puppy plenty of water throughout the day, especially around mealtime because this is critical for carrying waste material from his body.

Sleeping Schedule

Consistency in your puppy's sleeping patterns is also important. Crate training really comes in handy here. A puppy likes to keep his "den" clean, so he will be less likely to eliminate in his crate as long as it is not too big. You will learn more about crate training for housetraining later in this chapter.

You can predict that a puppy will almost always need to eliminate when he wakes up in the morning or after naps. He should be given an opportunity to eliminate before retiring to the crate for a nap or for the night.

Playtime

When a puppy engages in an exciting activity such as playtime, chances are he will need to eliminate during or afterwards. Keep your play sessions short and make sure you give him plenty of time to eliminate before coming back into the house.

Command Phrase

Think of a command phrase that you will say every time you want your dog to go outside. It could be "Do you want to go outside" or "Do you want to go potty?" You will use this same phrase every time you take him outside. Whatever phrase you decide to say, make sure you say it in a very upbeat, positive tone! You want your puppy to think that going outside is a very exciting activity.

Supervise

If you are constantly supervising your dog, accidents will happen less often. This is because you will be able to see "clues" such as sniffing around or walking in circles. If you can't be in the same room with your puppy, you can keep him in a crate, but not for long periods of time.

Don't Punish

All dogs will have accidents. Even after you think that he is fully housetrained, he will still have the occasional accident.

You should never punish your dog if you stumble upon an accident that happened a few hours ago. For example, if you call your dog to an accident and say "Rover, come" and point out a mess to him and scold him, he will think you are punishing him for coming, not the accident. If you do this, your dog may become fearful of you.

If you catch your dog in the act of eliminating, refrain from yelling or hitting him (even though you may want to!) Instead, use a verbal reprimand word or phrase such as "no," "eh-eh," or "hey" in a firm tone, but don't yell. This sound will interrupt his action and then you can take him outside.

You should also never punish a dog for submissive elimination. This could happen when your dog gets overly excited, if he gets scolded, or if there are visitors in the house. This is something that he will eventually outgrow, but until then, just be patient with him.

Clean Messes

When your dog has an accident in the house, clean the mess as soon as you can with a deodorizer to get rid of the odor. If you don't clean the area with a deodorizer, the odor will draw your dog back to that spot to eliminate.

You should also clean up your puppy's messes outside too. A clean environment is important for your puppy's health. Piles of feces on the lawn not only look and smell bad, but it can cause diseases from being infested with canine worm larvae. This can also prevent the habit of coprophagy (eating feces.) This will be discussed in Chapter 11.

Grant Freedom

As your dog has fewer accidents inside the house, you will be able to let him wander around the house more. Do this gradually. If he has accidents with this new freedom, go back to watching him closely until you he has proven himself again.

Deciding Which Method to Use

Before your new puppy arrives to your home, you should decide how you are going to housetrain him. There are several ways to housetrain your puppy. It is important to decide on a method and then stick with it for the duration of your dog's life. Changing methods will confuse your dog and will ultimately cause accidents. Apply the principles that you just learned to these methods.

You can train him to go outside, "paper" potty training, potty pads, or a litter pan. Once you make the decision, everyone in the family should be sure to train the same way.

How to Housetrain to Go Outside

Housetraining is teaching your dog to eliminate outside only—he is never allowed to eliminate indoors. From the moment you bring your new puppy or dog home, you want to take him immediately to the spot you want to designate as his "elimination area."

Use your command phrase "go outside" or "go potty." As soon as he eliminates, immediately give him verbal praise and a reward.

Anticipate his future needs to go outside by tracking his cycle as mentioned earlier. Whenever it is time to eliminate, take him outside and once again give the command phrase "go outside" or "go potty."

If your yard does not have a fence, or you live in an apartment, you will want to take your dog out on a leash. Attach the leash to the collar and say "Rover come" in an upbeat tone. When he begins to walk, praise him. Lead the puppy directly to where you want him to eliminate, and say use your command phrase. Otherwise, he may be confused and think you are taking him out for a walk.

He won't always eliminate on cue. In fact, you could spend several minutes outside waiting for him to eliminate. But until he is fully housetrained, you need to be there with him. Once he finally eliminates, give him immediate praise and a reward.

If you are taking your puppy to eliminate other than your own yard, make sure that you keep him from going on your neighbor's lawn, in public recreational areas, or children's playgrounds. Always take a plastic bag with you so you can pick up his feces and throw it away immediately into an outdoor trash can.

Female dogs squat to urinate, however, male dogs raise their hind legs and aim at vertical objects, or "targets." So, be aware of where your male dog chooses to urinate. Curbs, phone poles, and fire hydrants are acceptable locations. However, automobiles, bicycles, mailboxes, young trees, fences, plants, and shrubbery are not. If you see your dog striking the pose, gently tug on the leash and keep walking until you find an appropriate object.

Consistency is very important with housetraining. If you are not consistent with when you take him out and where you take him out, it will be hard for your dog to know what is right and what is wrong.

How to Paper Train

Paper training is when you train your puppy to eliminate on several layers of newspapers inside your house that are in the same spot at all times. Of course, you change the papers after each use, but the key is that the newspapers are always available for the puppy's use.

Paper training is separate from housetraining. It is not a preliminary step to housetraining. This is a common mistake among people. The only exception is for very young puppies that are too young to go outside. If you decide to teach your puppy paper training, it then should be used for the rest of his life.

Paper training is a practical method for:

- People who have a small dog and live in an apartment.

- People who are elderly, handicapped, or find it difficult to walk their dog.

- People who have young puppies with little or no control of their bladder or bowel muscles yet.

- People who have puppies that have not had all of their immunization shots yet.

- People who work long hours and must leave their dogs home alone.

If you paper train a puppy to go inside with the intentions of eventually training him to go outside, he will be very confused. Especially, when the change is gradual. If you must make the switch, it is better to do it all at once, that way he knows that the paper way has been replaced with going outside. Otherwise, he might not go outside, but instead go inside where his papers are—or used to be!

When you paper train, select a quiet corner in the kitchen or a bathroom. Make sure that this is a room that you don't mind being his permanent elimination area. The location should not be in a high-traffic area. After all, everyone likes their privacy!

Cut a plastic trash bag in an approximate 3 x 4-foot area and lay it where you want your puppy to eliminate. Next, lay 6 to 8 sheets of newspaper over the plastic bag and tape down the corners. After awhile, your puppy will recognize this as his elimination area and you can start making the space smaller.

It is essential that you lay the papers down in the same area every time. You will take your puppy to this area when he wakes up in the morning, 15- 20 minutes after each meal, after each nap, after playtime, and before bedtime. Also, if he is ever showing signs such as excessive sniffing or walking around in circles, take him to the elimination area.

At the elimination area, give him his command "go potty" in a pleasant tone of voice. If he wanders off, place him back on the papers. Once he goes, praise him and reward him.

One your puppy has become comfortable eliminating on the papers, then you can start using the "come" command. Whenever it is time for him to go, such as first thing in the morning or after a meal, walk to the papers and say "Rover, come." He will then know that it is time for him to eliminate.

If your puppy starts having accidents off of the paper, you should start the paper training process over again.

How to Train with Potty Pads

Potty training pads are also used for indoor training. These are absorbent pads that are scientifically treated to attract a puppy to eliminate on it. You can use the same steps for the potty pads as you do paper training. The benefit to potty pads is that it absorbs moisture so you can easily throw it away after use. Additionally, these are easy to travel with if you will be staying in a hotel, on a boat, etc.

How to Train with a Litter Pan

Another indoor training method is litter pan training. This is when you train a small dog to eliminate in a cat litter pan. The main benefit to this method over paper training is that a tray filled with kitty litter or shredded newspapers is not as unsightly as soiled newspapers. A heavy-duty plastic pan is best because it can be washed easily with soap and hot water.

The basic concept of litter plan training is the same as paper training. To make the pan more appealing to your puppy, place a newspaper shred with his urine on it in the pan. Or, leave a small piece of feces in the pan. He will be drawn by his scent. Let him sniff around, place him in the pan, and say a command such as "Rover, go potty" or "Rover, use your tray." When he eliminates, praise him.

If he doesn't eliminate, place him back into his crate for 5 to 10 minutes, then carry him to the pan again. Repeat this until he goes.

Remove the soiled papers from the pan immediately after use and flush solid waste down the toilet.

Other Housetraining Methods

There are other housetraining methods that can be used too. These are the "bell" and "speak" methods.

Bell Method

The bell method is just what it sounds like—using a bell to indicate when your dog has to go outside. Simply hang a string of bells on the door handle of the door he uses to go outside. Lower it to his level so he can easily reach it. Then, every time you go to take him outside, take his paw or nose and jiggle the bells. Once you repeat this several times, he will understand that the bells are there for him to indicate that he needs to go outside.

There are some disadvantages to using the bell method. For one, many dogs prefer to play with the bells, so it is hard to tell if your dog really needs to go out, or if he is just entertaining himself.

Second, the bells might not be able to be heard from all over the house. This actually defeats the purpose of having the bells if you can't hear it from every room.

Third, if you are traveling, you will need to take the bells with you.

Speak on Command

This method is beneficial when your dog is already housetrained. When you are at the door to take him outside, say "Rover, do you need to go outside?" or "Rover, do you need to go potty?" Then say, "Can you speak?" When he barks, say "Yes, good boy" and open the door.

You can do the same thing for going back into the house. Be aware though, some dogs think that you are actually playing a game. For example they may "speak" when you just had him outside. In this case, you need to pay close attention to his elimination schedule.

Housetraining will be one of your most proud accomplishments with your dog! It takes a lot of work and a lot of patience, but you will feel a great sense of "relief" when your dog is housetrained!

In Chapter 11 you will learn about some common behavioral problems and how they can be fixed.

Chapter 11:
Common Behavioral Problems

If you have been doing basic and even advanced obedience training with your dog, but he still misbehaves in other ways, you need to learn how to fix the problems before they spin out of control.

Such bad behaviors include chewing, digging, barking, jumping up, chasing, begging, and biting. Your dog doesn't perform these bad behaviors to make you mad—he just doesn't know that they are bad unless you teach him!

Many dog owners do not take the initiative to correct such behavioral problems. So, they give up hope on their dog and send them to a shelter. This can be avoided with proper training.

This chapter will help you learn how to handle aggression, chewing, digging, barking, jumping up, begging, mounting, biting/nipping, running away, chasing cars, traveling problems, coprophagy, and separation anxiety.

1. Aggression

You already learned a little about aggression and animal aggression in Chapter 5 – Temperament, but it is important enough to be discussed in greater detail in this chapter.

Aggressive behavior is normal for dogs in their own environment—after all they are descendants of the wolf. Dogs communicate by biting, growling, showing teeth, and snarling and this is perfectly normal for them. But, this behavior is not acceptable among humans—especially in the home.

Ironically, most dogs become aggressive because their human owners have not properly trained or socialized the dogs.

Aggression towards Humans

Aggression can be triggered by humans in a variety of ways. For example, maybe a child is so excited to see her dog that she squeezes him as hard as she can with a big hug. The dog probably won't interpret this as a loving gesture, but rather a threat. Therefore, he could strike back.

A dog could also show aggression if he is confused about the hierarchy of your family. He needs to have a clear understanding that he is below everyone including small children. It this is not clear, he could test his authority.

A dog can also become aggressive if someone is taunting or teasing him with his food bowl, toys, or other possessions. What may seem like innocent fun could be rather alarming to the dog.

When someone or another animal is invading his territory, the dog could become aggressive by barking, biting, or urinating. When someone is threatening a dog physically and he feels pain, the dog will do what he needs to do to defend himself—which is usually the act of biting back.

Aggression towards Other Pets

When there is more than one pet in the family, it is important that they play well with each other. If they are aggressive with each other, it could cause very serious situations down the road.

A dog will show aggression towards another household pet when the two have been playing rough or playing too long with each other. The dogs could also growl or bark at another dog walking outside the house or while on a walk. Because they can't reach the other dog (because they are inside or on a leash), they could attack each other.

Predation is another common aggressive behavior among dogs when they are competing for food. This is why it is a good idea to make sure they each have their own food bowl.

Managing Aggression

When a dog shows signs of aggression, you need to be very careful with how you try to manage it. Barking or growling is a sign of emotion, so you don't want to punish him for doing this. Because if he doesn't bark before possibly striking, you won't have a warning!

Punishing the dog when he is in fear will only make him more fearful and more aggressive. **When you see the signs of aggression, there are several ways to help manage it:**

- Keep your dog on a leash whenever he is around other people or other dogs, even indoors.

- Do not punish your dog by hitting, kicking, pulling, or yelling at him.

- Try to avoid the situation in which your dog previously showed aggression.

- Do not force your dog to interact with people or other dogs if he is shy. It will need to be a gradual process.

- If your dog is on a leash and growling or barking as you approach other dogs or people, don't stop to socialize.

- Use a head collar or muzzle around other people and dogs in which he has shown aggression.

- It is worthwhile considering visiting your Vet for a physical checkup of your dog to rule out any physical cause of pain that may be causing your dog's aggression.

- While spaying or neutering does not cause an overall personality change, it may help reduce your pet's irritability and moodiness by reducing its hormones as a result of the surgery. Neutering or spaying your dog may decrease your dog's "dominance" tendency which could be causing the aggression. Additionally it may also have a positive effect on reducing territorial aggression and wandering. It can takes a month or more after the surgery for any change to be noticed and improvement is not achieved in all cases.

- Time out can be used by placing your dog in a secluded are for 5 about minutes or so immediately after displaying any aggression. As mentioned earlier dogs enjoy human companionship and will soon learn to associate their aggressive behavior with a negative outcome.

Of course, if none of these techniques help manage your dog's aggression, you should consult with a professional trainer.

A Special Note about Children and Dogs

You've read about children and dogs throughout this E-book, but it is important to highlight the subject because children are more likely to be bitten by dogs than adults.

Children and dogs can make wonderful playmates. However, unless they know how to play with each other nicely, the situation could become very dangerous.

Dogs bite for many different reasons, as you read in the "Aggression" sections above. Small children are very intrigued by dogs. They love to pull on tails, tug at ears, and wrestle with them!

Older children might see what teasing and taunting they can get away with. These types of situations frighten the dog and he could therefore strike back with a bite. A dog bite can be very deep and damaging to a child's skin. In rare and extreme cases, it could even cause death.

People usually assume that a child is more likely to get bit by a stray dog; however, a child is actually more likely to get bitten by a dog that he knows—either a family pet or a neighbor's dog.

There are things you can do to prevent your child (or someone else's child) from receiving a dog bite:

- Don't leave your dog alone with young children—even your own children. As your children get older and you gain confidence in your dog, then you can allow them to play alone together.

- Don't assume that just because you have a dog breed that is known to be good with children, that your dog is actually good with children if he has not grown up with them. All dogs need to be conditioned gradually to children.

- Don't let children (or adults) taunt, tease, hit, kick, or poke your dog.

- Don't let children yell or act too rowdy around dogs.

- Don't let your dogs go near strange dogs.

If you provide constant supervision to your children and your dogs, you should be able to prevent aggressive dog behavior before it arises.

2. Chewing

It is very common for puppies to chew when they are teething. The act of chewing helps their teeth break through the gums. Older dogs, generally chew if they are bored or anxious.

If a dog is bored, it is because he has built up so much energy, but has run out of ways to exert it. So he finds something interesting to chew.

The only problem is, is that he doesn't know what is permissible to chew unless you have taught him. So the sooner you teach him, the less likely he will chew your household items. A dog may also chew if he has been left alone and not within the comfort of his own crate. This is known as a "spite chewer." He is upset that you have left him so he will start chewing as soon as you leave.

By keeping your dog in a crate when you leave your house, you are not "punishing" him, rather you are keeping him in a safe and comfortable environment. You can place lots of fun chew toys in the crate to keep him occupied while you are away. If you don't keep him in a crate while you are gone and instead let him roam about, he will help himself to chew on anything he wants!

When you return home to find that your dog is in the act of chewing something he shouldn't be, give a sharp "no," but do not yell. Take the object away and ignore him for five to ten minutes. If you start to play with him or feed him, he will think he is being rewarded for the chewing.

If you don't catch your dog in the act of chewing, don't scold your dog, but instead ignore him. Some trainers recommend that you pick up the destroyed object and look at it angrily. However, you don't want your dog to misinterpret that as you are upset with him (even though you are!)

Prevent Chewing

There are some proactive steps you can take to help eliminate the act of chewing. These steps can be used by puppies and adult dogs.

- **Puppy-proof** – As you learned earlier in this E-book, you need to puppy-proof your home. Even if your dog is older, you still need to take precautions to make potentially-destructive objects out of your dog's reach.

- **Provide Toys** – Make sure your dog has a plentiful selection of chew toys available to him at all times.

- **Provide Sound** – Instead of turning off the television or radio when you leave the house, turn them on. The extra background noise will help your dog feel more at ease.

- **Increase Exercise** – Providing your dog with frequent exercise will help him burn off excess energy that he could otherwise use towards items in your home.

Correct Chewing

It is your responsibility to initiate training to correct your dog's chewing problem. Practice this training by placing some inappropriate objects on the floor, such as a book, a shoe, etc.

As he approaches the inappropriate object, give the "leave it" command that you learned in Chapter 8. Take the object away and replace it with a chew toy or bone. Once the dog starts chewing the chew toy or bone, praise him.

Practice this training exercise several times a day with many different inappropriate objects.

3. Digging

Dogs dig for a variety of reasons. Some dogs find digging a very natural activity. For example, dachshunds were bred to go down holes, so digging seems perfectly normal to them.

Other dogs may dig outside because they want to bury something, they want to build a shelter, they dig a hole to eliminate in, or probably most commonly—they dig because they are bored!

Some dogs dig inside the house too. Perhaps they will dig once they have found a comfortable spot on the carpet or sofa. This may not look like much destruction in the beginning, but it won't take long for the digging to really show!

Prevent Digging

There is not a lot you can do to puppy-proof the inside of your house from digging (you can't really remove your carpet and furniture!) But you can take measures outside.

If you have flowers or a garden that you don't want destroyed, fence them off. Fence off any areas that you don't want your dog to dig in.

Give your dog plenty of exercise and playtime to exert his energy. The more activities you provide him with, the fewer activities— such as digging—that he will have to find on his own.

Correct Digging

As with chewing, you should not punish your dog for digging if you were not there to see it. However, if you catch him in the act, say "no" and remove him from the situation. Give him something else to do so he doesn't go back to digging.

4. Barking

Barking is a perfectly natural canine behavior. Birds sing; frogs croak; and a dog barks, whines and howls. If you have a dog, you should expect some barking, whining or howling.

It is unrealistic and unfair to think you can train your dog to stop barking altogether. However, you, your neighbors and your dog will all be much happier if the barking is under control.

If your dog is an excessive barker, you need to find out what he is barking about—which is not always easy.

Your dog may be barking excessively because you unintentionally trained her to do so. Poochie speaks and you obey. "Woof" and you open the door to let puppy out, "woof" and you open it again to let her in. "Woof" and she gets a treat, "woof" when you come home from work. Your dog has learned to get attention through barking.

The first step in obtaining peace and quiet is to realize that barking is often caused by your dog being lonely, bored, frustrated, frightened or seeking your attention. These are all situations that you can help to alleviate. A well-exercised, happy dog is more likely to sleep all day while you are not home.

Prevent Barking

Below are some tips that you can do prevent excessive barking from your dog, including:

- **Use a leash** – If your dog is barking uncontrollably when you are home, keep him on a leash so you can say "no" easily.

- **Use a crate** – Send your dog to his crate for a 30 second time-out.

- **Provide Sound** – Drown out background noises that might frighten your dog with a television or radio.

- **Close the Curtains** – If there is a certain time of the day when you know people will be outside your house (for example, when the mail deliverer is making his rounds or when school children are walking to or from school), then shut the curtains.

- **Increase Exercise** – Allow him to burn off some of his energy by giving him frequent exercise such as a walk or following some of the commands he learnt during his Obedience Training in Chapter 7.

- **Adequately socialize your dog** – A well socialized dog is less likely to bark at every person, cat or dog in his vicinity.

Correct Barking

There are a few different corrective actions you can take to stop your dog from barking.

One thing you can do is use a command such as "no" or "quiet" when he is barking. As soon as he starts barking, say "no" or "quiet." As soon as he stops barking, praise him and reward him. If he immediately starts barking again, say "no" or "quiet" again. Repeat this as often as you need to.

If the command alone is not enough to keep your dog from barking, you will need to condition your dog not to bark. You can do this by pretending to go outside. Stay right on the other side of the door, and listen for your dog to bark. Then, when he starts barking, open the door quickly and say "no" or "quiet." Repeat this over and over again, until you can leave without him barking.

Another option is to ignore your dog when he is barking. He is barking because he wants your attention. When you give him attention, even if it is to give him a command, you are rewarding him with your attention. Therefore, when he is barking at you, turn your head the other way, or leave the room.

With all of these corrective actions, you need to be sure to praise your dog when he is not barking with a "good dog, yes, no bark!"

5. Jumping Up

It is very common for a dog to jump up on his owner or anyone who walks through the door! He is happy to see you and expresses it with a big "hello!"

So why does your dog keep jumping on you when you come home? Chances are you're happy to see him too, so you pet him, pick him up, or give him treats. In your dog's mind, these are rewards! You are rewarding him for jumping up on you!

When this happens use the "off" command and then "sit" as you learned in Chapter 7. To prevent your dog from jumping on you, do not pet him, pick him up, or give him treats upon your arrival—no matter how excited you are to see him too!

If he jumps on the sofa next to you and you don't want him there, don't pet him or give him attention. Instead, give the "off" command. Be sure to reward him with a treat once he is off.

6. Begging

Anyone who does not crate their dog while the family is eating a meal is familiar with begging! Sometimes you may give in and other times you may not.

This inconsistency will be really confusing for your dog. Therefore, it is best if you avoid feeding your dog at the table. If he does, say "no" and ignore him. Continue carrying on your dinner and conversation as normal. Your dog will continue to whine and bark, but just continue to ignore him. When he stops, praise him.

To avoid begging, it is a good idea to keep your dog in his crate while you are eating.

Give him something to keep him busy such as toys and treats.

7. Mounting

Mounting or "humping" is a behavior that is more commonly seen with male dogs than female dogs. However, some female dogs have been known to mount against their owner's leg as a way to challenge his authority.

Regardless of the reason for mounting—by male or female—it should be corrected immediately. Simply say "no," gently guide the dog off the leg or object, and divert him to another activity.

Watch your dog closely for this behavior so you can correct it every time you see it as this can be embarrassing for the dog owner and anyone in the dog's company.

8. Biting or Nipping

Many puppies bite or nip when they are playing. They did this with their littermates, so they will continue to do it with you unless you train him to stop.
Other possible causes of biting or nipping include fear, aggression (mentioned earlier in this chapter), physical pain caused by injury or illness (see your Vet if this is a possibility) , or jealousy.

Although it may not be painful for you, you need to teach your dog that this behavior is not acceptable.

There are several different ways you can deter this behavior. When he bites or nips, say "no" in a firm voice—but don't scold. Once he stops biting, praise him and reward him. If he resumes biting, say "no" again and this time leave the room. This will help him realize that biting doesn't gain your attention, instead he loses it.

Ensure you do not play any "tug of war" games with the puppy or dog that is nipping or biting. This only encourages the negative behavior. Another way to get your dog to stop biting is when he bites you, say "ouch, that hurt!" and act as if you are in pain. Your dog will feel very sad for hurting you and he will stop immediately.

If the biting or nipping is caused by an object that your dog had leaned to fear, try to slowly "desensitize" your dog to the object. For example if you dog nips you every time you try and groom him with a brush, spend some time playing with your dog using the brush as a toy and using a treat whenever he plays without nipping. The idea being that eventually your dog sees the brush is something that is fun to be around and that brings a positive reward with it.

If the nipping or biting is becoming more aggressive read the section on managing aggression in your dog in this chapter.

In certain cases you may need to consider a muzzle for your dog if there is concern for human safety, particularly for children's safety. If none of these options work for your dog, you should consult a professional trainer.

This way, you can stop the behavior before someone really gets hurt.

9. Running Away

No one wants their dog to run away, but there are several reasons that can cause it. Below you will learn the causes and management of running away.

- **Your dog is bored** – If your dog is bored, try increasing his exercise or including him in more family activities.

- **Your dog finds something more exciting outside** – If your dog sees children playing outside or other dogs, he will want to join them. When you notice this activity, keep your dog away from the windows or shut the curtains.

- **Your dog has a desire to mate** – Spaying and neutering will help prevent this urge.

- **Your dog has separation anxiety** – To prevent your dog from running away after you let him out of his crate, keep treats and toys inside to occupy his time. When you get home, give him some exercise or play time. You could also consider enrolling your dog in doggie day care.

- **Your dog has not been trained properly** – Review the "wait" command in Chapter 7.

10. Chasing

It is a natural instinct for a dog to chase anything that moves! This curiosity of his may be amusing to watch your dog chase a bug, but when he decides to chase a car or bus, it is a real problem—even when he is on a leash!

To prevent chasing, do not look at whatever has caught your dog's attention. If you do, it just reinforces that this object (whatever it may be) is very interesting. If you see your dog's ears perk up with interest, say "no." As soon as your dog looks away from the object, praise him. If the object is so interesting that "no" doesn't work, walk in the opposite direction.

This is much more difficult to do when your dog is not on the leash, so be sure to practice the "come" command from Chapter 7 often.

11. Traveling Problems

There will be times when you need to or want to travel with your dog. If you take some precautions, you can prevent common problems so your dog will have a more enjoyable journey.

The best thing you can do for your dog is to introduce him to traveling at an early stage. When he is young enough to come home with you, he should be young enough for traveling.

Car Rides

If the only time your dog rides in the car is to the veterinarian's office, he will probably show signs of fear as he approaches the car. You want your dogs to love car rides, so make them a reward!

When your dog has done something good reward him with a car ride. Say in a very enthusiastic tone, "Rover, do you want to go for a car ride?" Even if you only drive around your neighborhood, your dog will love the scenery—and will love it when you roll down his window so he can feel the nice breeze!

Some dogs get car sick, so shorter rides are best. If you know when you will be taking your dog for a car ride, avoid giving him food and water two hours beforehand. If he still gets sick, talk to your veterinarian about giving him motion sickness medicine before rides.

Airplane Rides

If you are planning an airplane trip and you want to bring your dog along, call the airline first to inquire about their pet policy. Every airline has different pet restrictions. Some airlines only allow dogs of a certain weight limit and other airlines don't allow dogs at all.

If you can take your dog on the plane, you need to make all the arrangements such as obtain a health certificate from your veterinarian, identification tags, etc. You all need to take precautions that your pet has a safe ride.

If your dog is small enough, he can stay in his carrying case and slipped under the seat in front of you. He will most likely cry or act scared.

Talk to your veterinarian about giving him motion sickness medicine beforehand. Also, refrain from giving him food and water to hours before your trip.

However, if you think your puppy gets thirsty during the trip, ask for some ice chips and feed those to him.

12. Coprophagy

Coprophagy is when a dog eats his own stool. This can be a shocking and disturbing behavior for a dog owner to see. This behavior is more common with puppies, and those puppies tend to outgrow it as they get older.

Veterinarians typically believe that coprophagy is caused by the way the puppy was treated before you brought him home. Perhaps he came from a puppy mill or pet store where he was not fed adequately. Extreme hunger, combined with an unclean cage could lead the puppy to eat his stool. It can also be caused if the puppy has a digestive enzyme deficiency.

Coprophagy can also be caused when a dog is stressed from a move, or frustrated or anxious. If a dog has been left alone for many hours at a time, for example, he could become irritated and take his frustration out by eating his waste.

There are several ways that you can prevent coprophagy. First, take your puppy to the veterinarian to test for nutritional deficiency. You may need to switch to a higher-quality dog food. If that doesn't solve the problem, go outside with your dog and pick up his stool as he defecates. If you happen to catch your dog in the act of eating, say "no" and remove him from the feces. Then, clean it up.

Another popular method to prevent coprophagy is to add meat tenderizer or pineapple juice to your puppy's food. The puppy will be deterred by the distasteful addition. As a last resort, you could start walking your puppy on a leash so you can direct where he walks.

13. Separation Anxiety

Separation anxiety can be a real problem for your dog. Not knowing where you are going or when you will be back can be very stressful for the dog. He could become anxious and even aggressive if he is left in his crate too long.

Signs of Separation Anxiety

There are many signs of separation anxiety including: barking, chewing, defecating, digging, excessive salivating, scratching, and urinating. Chewing, digging, and scratching are signs of your dog trying to "escape." Barking, defecating, excessive salivating, and urinating are signs of anxiety and fear.

Causes of Separation Anxiety

Such causes of separation anxiety include genetics, lack of socialization, lack of training, lack of confidence, mistreatment by a previous owner, extensive confinement, and too much bonding with the owner. As you can see, most of these are the owner's responsibility.

Treatment of Separation Anxiety

There are things that you can do to prevent separation anxiety. When you put your dog in his crate, don't have a long, emotional good-bye. Simply, walk away. It is even a good idea to ignore your dog 5 minutes before you leave. If you draw attention to your departure, your dog will worry when the love and emotion is suddenly stopped.

Also try and teach your dog not to associate certain behaviors of yours with your leaving the house and being away for hours. Dogs, as we have learnt in Chapter 1 are good at associating certain actions with certain outcomes. You may have noticed for example that as dress for work, or pick up your car keys, your dogs begins to get anxious.

Try changing your dog's negative associations to your behaviors to positive ones.

For example, on a weekend, dress for work, pick up the car keys and go outside for a few minutes only, then come back inside and give your dog a treat. You dog will eventually begin to associate you getting ready for work as a positive association rather than a negative one.

Make sure you have plenty of treats and toys in your dog's crate to keep him entertained while you are away. If your dog always knows that he'll have treats when you leave, it won't be as traumatic for him. Before you leave, turn on a radio or television so your dog has some noise. A talk station is more effective than music, because the sound of human voices could comfort him. You could even tape your own voice.

When you return home, don't give your dog any emotion or attention when you let him out of his crate. This will reinforce that being outside of the crate is better than being inside the crate. Let him outside to eliminate immediately.

In extreme causes a calmative type medication may be prescribed for you dog by your Vet.

Separation anxiety is something that should improve over time. However, if it does not, or if your dog shows signs of extreme aggression when he is let out, seek a professional trainer and/or see you Vet for further assistance.

When you pay close attention to your dog's behavior, you are better able to identify his bad behaviors and correct them through training exercises. Your dog wants your attention and love, so when use this to your advantage when you are training.

CONCLUSION

A dog can bring so much joy and love to you and your family. When you bring a dog into your home whether a brand new puppy or an older dog from a shelter—you are opening up your home and your heart to a wonderful new relationship.

Before bringing a dog into your home, it is your responsibility to do the research and take the steps to ensure that he will feel safe and comfortable. It is your responsibility to make sure that everyone is in agreement to a new dog and willing to help care for him.

It is also your responsibility to dedicate time to training. The amount and quality of training that your dog receives will have more of an impact on his behaviors and your relationship than anything else.

Training is not just a few weeks of intensive exercises. Rather it is a lifelong commitment that will benefit both you and your dog.

You won't regret the time and dedication you give to dog training. It will be a fantastic bonding experience that will strengthen your relationship. So now that you know the basics of dog training, it's time to begin!

Happy training!